C000082613

THE BIRTH OF HATRED

THE BIRTH OF HATRED
Developmental, Clinical, and Technical Aspects of Intense Aggression

edited by
SALMAN AKHTAR, M.D.
SELMA KRAMER, M.D.
and HENRI PARENS, M.D.

JASON ARONSON INC.
Northvale, New Jersey
London

Production Editor: Judith D. Cohen

This book was set in 12 point Bem by TechType of Upper Saddle River, New Jersey, and printed and bound by Haddon Craftsmen of Scranton, Pennsylvania.

Library of Congress Cataloging-in-Publication Data

The birth of hatred : development, clinical, and technical aspects of
    intense aggression / edited by Salman Akhtar, Selma Kramer, and
    Henri Parens.
        p. cm.
    Includes bibliographical references and index.
    ISBN 1-56821-428-6
    1. Hate. 2. Aggressiveness (Psychology) 3. Parent and child.
    4. Violence—Psychological aspects. I. Akhtar, Salman, 1946 July
    31– II. Kramer, Selma. III. Parens, Henri, 1928–   .
    BF575.H3B57 1995
    152.4—dc20   94-23614

Manufactured in the United States of America. Jason Aronson Inc. offers books and cassettes. For information and catalog write to Jason Aronson Inc., 230 Livingston Street, Northvale, New Jersey 07647.

To the memory

of

Margaret S. Mahler,

teacher, friend, source of inspiration

Contents

Acknowledgments

The chapters in this book were originally papers presented at the Twenty-fifth Annual Margaret S. Mahler Symposium on Child Development held on April 30, 1994, in Philadelphia. First and foremost, therefore, we wish to express our gratitude to the Margaret S. Mahler Psychiatric Research Foundation. We are also grateful to Troy L. Thompson II, M.D., Chairman, Department of Psychiatry and Human Behavior, Jefferson Medical College, as well as to the Philadelphia Psychoanalytic Institute and Society for their shared sponsorship of this symposium. Many colleagues from the Institute and Society helped during the symposium and we remain grateful to them. Finally, we wish to acknowledge our sincere appreciation of Ms. Maryann Nevin for her efficient organization of the symposium as well as pleasant and skillful assistance in the preparation of this book's manuscript.

Contributors

Salman Akhtar, M.D.
Professor of Psychiatry, Jefferson Medical College; Training and Supervising Analyst, Philadelphia Psychoanalytic Institute, Philadelphia, Pennsylvania.

Harold P. Blum, M.D.
Clinical Professor of Psychiatry, New York University School of Medicine; Executive Director, Sigmund Freud Archives; Training and Supervising Analyst, Psychoanalytic Institute, New York University Medical Center, New York.

Dorothy E. Holmes, Ph.D.
Associate Professor of Psychiatry, Howard University Hospital; Training and Supervising Analyst, Baltimore-Washington Psychoanalytic Institute, Washington, D.C.

Otto F. Kernberg, M.D.
Associate Chairman and Medical Director, Department of Psychiatry, New York Hospital–Cornell Medical Center

(Westchester Division); Training and Supervising Analyst, Columbia University Center for Psychoanalytic Training and Research, White Plains, New York.

Selma Kramer, M.D.
Professor of Psychiatry, Jefferson Medical College; Training and Supervising Analyst, Philadelphia Psychoanalytic Institute, Philadelphia, Pennsylvania.

Peter B. Neubauer, M.D.
Clinical Professor of Psychiatry, New York University Medical College; Editor, Psychoanalytic Study of the Child, New York.

Henri Parens, M.D.
Professor of Psychiatry, Jefferson Medical College; Training and Supervising Analyst, Philadelphia Psychoanalytic Institute, Philadelphia, Pennsylvania.

Fred Pine, Ph.D.
Professor of Psychiatry (Psychology), Albert Einstein College of Medicine, New York.

PARENTS' HATRED OF THEIR CHILDREN: AN UNDERSTUDIED ASPECT OF CROSS-GENERATIONAL AGGRESSION

Selma Kramer, M.D.

A comment made by a cherished associate many years ago seems an apt introduction to this book: "I have often wondered about wars. They are planned, even plotted, by old men in the safety of lush conference rooms. But they send their healthiest young men, their sons, to wage the wars." In my time, most young men went to war docilely if not happily. But with the war in Vietnam, things changed. The more educated among the young men refused to be a part of it for they saw no compelling reason to do so. More important, perhaps, they did not trust the older generation, which seemed all too ready to use them, to have them killed if necessary, instead of making use of mechanisms already in place to prevent wars. They questioned the integrity of national leaders and, in doing so, contributed to the downfall of at least one United States president.

With this aggressive push–pull across sociopolitical generations as a backdrop, let me turn to the more intricate aspects of aggression between parents and children. The Oedipus complex, in this context, is a well-defined and well-accepted concept in psychoanalytic theory. However, its descriptions, from Freud (1924) onward, have customarily emphasized the child's aggressive (and libidinal) impulses toward the parents. The other side of this issue—the parental hostility toward children—has largely been ignored. A brief discussion of this neglected area will set the stage for the chapters to follow in this monograph on hatred.

FROM ORDINARY PARENTAL AGGRESSION TO FILICIDE

"Ordinary parental aggression" is of necessity brought into play in normal and benevolent parent–child relationships. Starting with the practicing subphase (Mahler et al. 1975), infants and toddlers begin to test their newfound motor skills with pleasure, and seem drawn to activities that are potentially dangerous. Parental aggression, expressed in the usual "no-no" for distracting the child or in even stronger verbal disapproval, is necessary for the well-being of the child. Even more risky activities of the rapprochement-subphase child must be stopped by the parents who are ultimately acting on the child's own behalf (Parens 1987). Many of today's parents use "time-outs" very effectively and without inflicting punishment on the child.

Parental admonitions not only serve to change the direction of the child's impulsive or dangerous activities, but also function to build superego precursors and facilitate the development of autonomy. Blum and Blum (1990) say "the young child becomes increasingly aware of its own powers, its capacity to act upon itself and environment, with greater and more persistent intentionality . . .ultimately, however, autonomy must subserve not only individual exploration and innovation, but the regulation of behavior" (p. 585). I agree with their proposal that appropriate correction and discipline of a child are necessary for the development of a healthy ego and superego. The child's eventual ability to tolerate reasonable frustration, I feel, is a measure of appropriate ego growth. Some mothers and fathers, however, go far beyond appropriate discipline, correction, or verbal disapproval, resulting in serious damage to the child's body and mind.

Those who have pursued the issues at stake here include Steele and Kemp (1962), Rascovsky and Rascovsky (1972), Atkins (1970), Steele (1970), and Shengold, whose many publications since 1963 culminated in the book, *Soul Murder* (1989). Steele (1970) differentiates parents who physically abuse their children from parents who sexually abuse them. For the most part, children are more often physically abused by their mothers and sexually abused by their fathers. However, more maternal sexual abuse has been reported in recent years (Kramer and Akhtar 1991). Most of these authors point out the confusion in the minds of children who are abused. Such children feel that parents must be right and they themselves wrong. If the child dares to complain, even in his own mind, "he feels enormously confused, in fact, split—innocent and culpable at the same time—and the confidence in the testimony of his own senses is broken" (Ferenczi 1933, p. 162).

In speaking of filicide in conjunction with wars, I address a phenomenon occurring for the most part between adolescent sons and their middle-aged fathers.[1] Psychoanalysis has leaned heavily upon the Oedipus myth in order to understand the intrapsychic development of the young child with lesser emphasis on similar reverberations in adolescence. The Rascovskys (1972), for instance, say that the Oedipus com-

---

1. A mother, too, may hate a preadolescent son to the point where she is driven to send him to a military prep boarding school. I was consulted by one such family recently.

plex should be buried after it has existed, because every
evolutionary possibility is kindled in the emotional forge of
filicide, parricide, and incest. Only the positive parental introjection can lead to repression. The Oedipus complex, if repressed, is the main foundation of human development, but if
unrepressed, is the basis of excessive acting out and psychopathic behavior.

The Rascovskys go on to state that repression of the
Oedipus complex fails when it is not counterbalanced by
positive parental introjections. This seems correct. However,
these authors fail to take into account the reemergence of the
Oedipus complex in adolescence when the father can no
longer physically or emotionally abuse his son. They also fail
to acknowledge that the Oedipus complex is never so completely repressed that its emergence in one's son may not be
cause for alarm, hatred, and the desire to kill the now taller,
stronger son. Brody (1970) says that

> It is no wonder that the dramatic struggle for power in the
> adolescent period may have an unconscious determinant dis-
> cernible in the beating fantasy, for in a more real way than
> before in his life the adolescent has the physical potential to be
> the active beater of the parent. The connections between
> reawakened fantasies of sexual brutality and reawakened fears
> of passive childlike surrender in the adolescent is obvious
> enough. The sadomasochistic complementations of parent and
> child need to undergo radical revisions, and both feel them-
> selves to be stepping on dangerous thresholds. The threat to
> both may be reduced eventually only by flight or by further
> displacements of active and passive positions to non-familial
> objects and *to the next generation*. [p. 446, emphasis added]

Rangell (1970) also speaks of the competitive jealousy
that often emanates from the parent toward the child of the
same sex. Anthony (1982) agrees and states that the child's

parricidal wish is paralleled by the generally unconscious wish in the father to destroy his son. Such destructiveness might take diverse forms and injure the spirit irreparably. Ross (1982) feels that one must be attentive to phenomena such as the *Laius complex* (i.e., the father's rivalry with and hostility toward the child) in order to understand cross-generational hatred.

Colarusso (1990) extends Mahler's developmental theory, to the mid-life crises that fathers must deal with in facing their adolescent sons' increasing sexual prowess. At the same time such a father is also concerned with losses inherent in his own middle age as well as the mental and physical deterioration of *his* parents.

In *Psychoanalytic Terms and Concepts*, Moore and Fine (1990) offer a succinct description of the classical Oedipus myth:

> The classic myth, as rendered in Sophocles' *Oedipus Rex*, tells of Laius, king of Thebes, who was warned by an oracle that a son yet to be born would kill him. When Jocasta, the Queen, gave birth to a boy, the king ordered that the infant be exposed to die on a mountainside. A shepherd found the infant and brought him to King Polybus, who adopted the boy. As a young man, Oedipus left Corinth and chanced to meet Laius at a crossroads; in a quarrel about the right-of-way, he slew the king, his father. Oedipus next came to the Sphinx, who blocked the road to Thebes and challenged every traveler to answer a riddle or die. Oedipus mastered the riddle and the Sphinx jumped to her death in mortification. The grateful Thebans made Oedipus king and married him to Jocasta. However, the gods would not tolerate incest, even without conscious participation, and plague fell upon Thebes. According to the oracle, finding the murderer of Laius was the price for lifting the plague. As Sophocles' play unfolds, Oedipus, sworn to uncover the crime and thus save the city, finds he is the murderer, married to his own mother. In the tragic

ending, Jocasta hangs herself and Oedipus blinds himself with
the brooch used to fasten her dress. [p. 134]

This depiction of the classical Oedipus myth reveals that
it was Laius who planned the murder of his 3-day-old son
after an oracle predicted that a not-yet-born son would kill
him. Presumably Oedipus did not know that the man he killed
at the crossroads was his father (see also Ross 1982) nor that
the woman given to him in marriage, Jocasta, was his mother
(Shengold 1989, pp. 41–68). Shengold, like Abse (1974) before him, also points out that mutilation of Oedipus' ankles
before being banished to die caused a severe deformity; it even
gave him the name Oedipus, that is, clubfoot.

While I focus on fathers who send their sons to war (to
death!), it is Shengold who should be credited for pointing out
that mothers too can be soul murderers. Even more than
having to maintain an image of the father as "good," it is
imperative for the child's mental well-being that he consider
the mother "good." "Consciously, however, the bad mother
is denied, in an effort to distance the overwhelming trauma"
(Shengold 1989, p. 64). This became apparent to me in the
following case.

Case 1

Donald's mother was psychotic with a strong paranoid
flavor. During his analysis, Donald reported that his mother
often appeared in his room scantily clad, to "adjust his air
conditioner" and was seductive in many other ways. However, it was not until late in analysis that he accused me of
knowing but not telling him that his nose and lips were getting
larger and smaller. He also felt that I was smiling at him in a
sarcastic fashion (a habit of his mother mentioned in the
analysis long ago). I then made a reconstruction, telling
Donald that someone indeed had had access to his body, and

had smiled sarcastically knowing that a part of his body (not his nose or lips) was changing size. In response, Donald said, "I really knew this all the while! My mother bathed me until I was 14, scrubbing all of me. I would get an erection and as soon as she left I would masturbate and feel so dirty again!" Donald's mother also called him ugly and said that she did not know how I could bear to look at him. Donald's father contributed to his soul murder by being unable to rescue him from the mother's sexual and verbal abuse. He seemed to fear Donald's desire to have friends and was very troubled when Donald began to date.

Atkins (1970)[2] refers to Friedenberg (1959) who says,

There is an obvious something in adolescence itself that both troubles and titillates many adults. The "teenager" seems to have replaced the communist as the appropriate target for public controversy and foreboding, for discussions designed less to clarify what is going on than to let people vent their fearful or hostile feelings and to declare themselves on the side of order and authority. [p. 176]

Atkins (1970) compared the need of the adolescent to deal with external and internal forces that affect his life's direction with the confrontation at the crossroads between Oedipus and Laius. Atkins questions whether it is possible that this confrontation at the crossroads "not only reflects Oedipus' struggle with his projected hatred returning in the form of superego prohibitions, but is also an example of the introjection of parental sadism and restraints manifest toward him from the beginning of his life?" (p. 862). Atkins also stresses Freud's (1924) and indeed most psychoanalysts' de-emphasis of the role that parental attitudes play in the formation and

2. I am thankful to Rachel Parens for bringing this reference to my attention.

development of the Oedipus complex. He refers to Rangell (1955), who pointed to parental aggression toward the child, which is self-evident in the unashamed authoritarian world and is consciously utilized by rulers and manipulators of power. Atkins chides psychoanalysis for focussing on the incestuous and parricidal child while ignoring the incestuous and filicidal impulses of the parent.

Atkins emphasizes that filicidal wishes may be both maternal and paternal. Our daily newspapers are convincing as they reveal the abuse, neglect, and even murder of infants and young children by parents. He says, however, that "parental aggression that was held in abeyance as long as the child was helpless, dependent, controllable, and a vessel for parental narcissism tends to be activated and neutralized and may break through with the onset of puberty." (p. 868). Parens (personal communication, July 1994) addresses questions concerning filicidal wishes on the part of female parents, and although she recognizes that at this point in history it is mainly male leaders and legislators who send mostly male children to war, she notes that Electra sets Orestes up for matricide every time. Parens proposes that the other side of murder and incest is rescue and suggests that this can explain defenses on the part of normal neurotic women that enable them to be helpful to other women and for normal neurotic men to be helpful to other men, that is, for each sex to be helpful in an altruistic way to members of the same sex. Regretfully, this successful defense fails all too often.

FATHERS WHO HATE

Not all fathers would willingly sacrifice their sons by sending them to war. Only some do. Who are they? I feel that fathers who had suffered abuse (hostility, indifference, constant criticism, and physical abuse) from their own fathers are unable to relate to their sons in a different way. The following cases illustrate this intergenerational dynamic well.

Case 2

Michael, age 9, was referred to me with the chief complaints of poor school work, stammering, verbal battles with his father (who abused him physically) and verbal and physical battles with his younger brother (whom he could best in any fight), many of which Michael himself provoked. Michael was the eldest child. He had two younger sisters whom his father idealized, and a younger brother who was badgered by both Michael and his father.

The father, Dr. Z., said that he did not know why, but he was incapable of treating his sons decently. It grieved him to acknowledge that he hated Michael and often wished that he had never been born. He seemed surprised when I asked him how he and *his* father got along. He burst out, "He hated me! I was never good enough for him, and he predicted that I never would be a success. But he loved my sister." Michael's grandfather had been an internationally famous specialist in his field of medicine and Michael's father entered the identical medical specialty. Dr. Z. told me that he was sure that Michael would end up being an auto mechanic.

Michael had had good mothering, which gave him an advantage that many male patients so badly fathered do not have. He expressed anger toward her for giving birth to the succession of his siblings. He said, "It's like the Chinese people. They have so many children that you can't win a war against them. Even if you killed those at the front of the line, there would be a never-ending line of soldiers to kill you." He hated, feared, and disdained his father, and at the same time yearned that his father would become a good father and that he could be a good son. Michael did well in his analysis, terminating at age 14.

I ran into Michael's father about 10 years later. He greeted me with ambivalence, which I understood, and he said, "Do you know what that S.O.B. did to me?" I told him that I was curious about Michael and I did not know what he had done to his father. Dr. Z. said, his face contorted with pain and anger, "He went through medical school and is taking a residency in my field. I wanted to send him to military school but my wife insisted that I let him go to college and medical school." Dr. Z., despised by his own father and left with distant relatives, when his parents took his sister to Europe, wished to send his eldest child to "live with strangers" who would prepare him for military service! Dr. Z., who was poorly fathered, could not be a better father even after Michael became a better son!

Case 3

Mr. N. consulted me because of a strain in his otherwise happy marriage: his wife wished for children and he did not. I asked him to describe his feelings about children. In response, he said, "I'm afraid to be a father. I may be like my own father, who terrified me. After dinner he worked on his stamp collection, closed up in his library, and then he'd stomp downstairs to my room to find out if I had done my homework right and it never was right. He'd holler, even scream, and once in a while he'd slap me. Suppose I do that!" I sent him to a colleague for therapy. I don't know what transpired in the therapy, but in about two years he called to announce the birth of a daughter. He was an overindulgent father, possibly able to be a better father to a daughter than to a son; possibly he was using such reaction formation that permitted him to be a parent; and possibly he could now love his daughter as he had wished that he and his father could love each other.

CONCLUSION

In agreement with my proposals in this chapter, Atkins (1970) says,

Just as revolution must be viewed as an expression of parricide, one final manifestation of parental filicidal aggression comes with the advent of our periodic wars between nations. The opportunity for massacre of the young assumes here its ultimate and most devastating form, and the blind kings of every household have their chance to act out and at the same time deny their own filicidal aggression. [p. 872]

Atkins asks a most important question: Are we as psychoanalysts significant help to a world which persists in destroying its young if we continue in remaining blind to the filicide which resides within all of us? My own modest attempt here is aimed at heightening the awareness of parental hostility toward children. The following contributions by Blum, Kernberg, and Pine, their respective discussions by Parens, Akhtar, and Holmes, and the concluding commentary by Neubauer should further enhance our understanding of the phenomenon of hatred in its myriad forms.

REFERENCES

Abse, D. W. (1974). Hysterical conversion and dissociative syndromes and the hysterical character. In *American Handbook of Psychiatry*, vol. 3, ed. S. Arieti and E. B. Brodie, 2nd ed., pp. 155–194. New York: Basic Books.

Anthony, J. B. (1982). Afterword. In *Father and Child*, ed. S. Cath, A. R. Gurwitt, and J. M. Ross, pp. 569–575. Boston: Little, Brown.

Atkins, N. B. (1970). The oedipal myth: adolescence and the succession of generations. *Journal of the American Psychoanalytic Association* 18:860–875.

Blum, E. J. and Blum, H. (1990). The development of autonomy and superego precursors. *International Journal of Psycho-Analysis* 71:585–595.

Brody, S. (1970). A mother is being beaten. In *Parenthood*, ed. J. Anthony and T. Benedek, pp. 427–446. Boston: Little, Brown.

Colarusso, C. (1990). The third individuation. *Psychoanalytic Study of the Child* 45:179–190. New Haven, CT: Yale University Press.

Ferenczi, S. (1933). Confusion of tongues between the adult and the child. In *Final Contributions to the Problems and Methods of Psychoanalysis*, pp. 156–167. London: Hogarth Press, 1955.

Friedenberg, E. Z. (1959). *The Vanishing Adolescent*, pp. 176–177. Boston: Beacon Press, 1966.

Freud, S. (1924). The dissolution of the oedipus complex. *Standard Edition* 19:173–179.

Kramer, S., and Akhtar, S. (1991). *The Trauma of Transgression: Psychotherapy of Incest Victims.* Northvale, NJ: Jason Aronson.

Mahler, M. S., Pine, F., and Bergman, A. (1975). *The Psychological Birth of the Human Infant.* New York: Basic Books.

Moore, B. E., and Fine, B. D. (1990). *Psychoanalytic Terms and Concepts.* New Haven, CT: Yale University Press.

Parens, H. (1987). *Aggression in our Children.* Northvale, NJ: Jason Aronson.

Rangell, L. (1955). The role of the parent in the oedipus complex. *Bulletin of the Menninger Clinic* 19:9–15.

––––––– (1970). The return of the repressed "oedipus." In *Parenthood*, ed. J. Anthony and T. Benedek, pp. 325–334. Boston: Little, Brown.

Rascovsky, A., and Rascovsky, M. (1972). Prohibition of incest, filicide and the sociocultural process. *International Journal of Psycho-Analysis* 53:271–276.

Ross, J. M. (1982). Oedipus revisited: Laius and the "Laius complex." *Psychoanalytic Study of the Child* 37:169–200. New Haven, CT: Yale University Press.

Shengold, L. (1989). *Soul Murder: The Effects of Childhood Abuse and Deprivation.* New Haven, CT: Yale University Press.

Steele, B. F. (1970). Parental abuse of infants and small children. In *Parenthood*, ed. J. Anthony and T. Benedek, pp. 449–477. Boston: Little, Brown.

Steele, B., and Kemp, C. H. (1962). The battered child syndrome. *Journal of the American Medical Association* 181:17–24.

2

SANCTIFIED AGGRESSION, HATE, AND THE ALTERATION OF STANDARDS AND VALUES

Harold P. Blum, M.D.

History confirms that there have always been human tendencies for release of aggression and mob violence, social sanctions for degradation, brutality, and sadomasochistic cruelties, and national sanctions and support for war. Even while espousing peace, people have an affinity for, and even a love of, war. Montaigne believed that society suffered from the ills of a long peace, and Kant stated,

> A long peace favors the predominance of a mere commercial spirit and with it a debasing self-interest, cowardice, and effeminacy, and tends to degrade the character of the nation. . . . War itself has something sublime about it and gives nations that carry it on in such a manner a stamp of mind only that [the] more sublime the more numerous the dangers to which they are exposed and which they are able to meet with fortitude. [Greenson 1963, p. 127]

VIOLENCE AND WAR

War is often glorified, and it appeals to national as well as personal narcissicism. War casts everyone into the polarized categories of friend or foe, virtuous or wicked, good or evil. We reward our military heroes with medals of honor, and we disparage those reluctant to fight as cowardly, effeminate, or unpatriotic. The group's collective superego sweeps away previous rules and regulations and substitutes its own moral judgments and values (Freud 1921). This group approval contributes to the contagious character of group aggression, hatred, and social violence. The group leader, so often charismatic and appealing, permits and promotes violence toward the debased "outsiders," and may seek to dehumanize a scapegoat or target group.

In Nazi Germany, the Aryans took the place of the biblical Jews as the "chosen people" of the führer-god. The leader is also a chosen person, usually endowed with grandiosity and omnipotence. Paranoid dictators have been both megalomanic and murderous. However irrational, the idealized leader and messianic message appealed to individual and national narcissism. By identifying with the leader and being only one member of the group, personal responsibility and personal guilt or shame are diminished. With group sanction, the individual is shameless, and adherence to the leader and to the group's values is rewarded while dissent is punished.

There is a special relationship between the leader and the led. The leader helps to define and organize the group but also responds to the aspirations and influence of the group. The leader may lead the group to where it has chosen to go. There is a relationship between the destructive pied piper and the childlike adults who blindly follow or co-determine this path to destruction. The identification with the idealized leader and group also confers a sense of belonging and a new identity. As in hypnosis, cognitive judgments and evaluations are delegated to the leader, who also takes on the role of commanding parent; the leader issues new commandments and espouses new injunctions and ideals. The group becomes the agency that approves and disapproves, superseding the personal superego in varying degree. The previous identity and ideals are submerged in the repressive pull of the group. The new family to which one has a sense of belonging and in which one has acquired a new identity is invested with feelings of allegiance and alliance, protection and security. Violence in war promotes comradeship, interdependence, willingness to sacrifice for the cause, and common ideals.

The regression that sets in with the hypnotic-like surrender to the leader and to the collective standards and values of the group superego accounts for the childlike thinking and emotion of the members of the group. Shared fantasies of power and glory, family and friendship are associated with identification with each other and the leader. Shared fantasies are embodied in social and national myths. Great orators, including demagogues, know how to appeal to infantile hunger for love and narcissistic supplies. Demagogues also appeal to the base instincts, to attitudes of destruction and hostility, and to sanctions for aggressive behavior and violence. The violence is typically directed to outsiders, preserving group bonding and cohesion. The violence may be sought as a form of direct participation or indirectly experienced through identification with the group. Hitherto prohibited gratifications are allowed to be expressed and experienced. Sadomasochistic and aggressive impulses and aggrandized violence are no longer restrained, but released. Through "holy wars," violence and murder are sanctified and exalted, as occurred in the crusades and their modern analogues. In the escalation to war, the sacrifice of the sons in battle by their oedipal fathers, and "macho" defense against femininity are powerful dynamics. We are aware of the significance of preoedipal aggression and envy in the predisposition to violence. Infantile helplessness and weakness, childhood traumata, child abuse and neglect, and feelings of being unloved and unlovable and of insignificance and inferiority mobilize and intensify rage and hatred.

HATE

Hatred is a complex, affective state alloyed with aggression that is not easy to define. Hatred is not the opposite of love, though hatred may be erotized. Hatred is the negative pole of ambivalence and coexists with narcissistic and object love. Freud (1915) postulated that hatred was an ego response and stated, "The ego hates, abhors, and pursues with intent to destroy all objects which are a source of unpleasurable feeling for it" (p. 138). In Freud's statement, hate is an ego attitude with the intent of destructive aggression. Hatred may be mobilized by need, fear, and frustration and by all unpleasant and noxious experiences. Transient or enduring, it tends to be closely linked to disturbance in psychic structure when hatred is intense, unremitting, and a motive force. Hatred requires sufficient ego development for persistent affective states associated with differentiation of self and object representations. The extreme form of hatred that Freud described, with its intent to destroy the object, is on a spectrum with the preservation of the object while making the object suffer and with the still milder form of coercion and control over a subjugated object. Hatred may characterize or merely color self and object relations.

A preponderance of love over hate is necessary for the attenuation of ambivalence and the development of object constancy. Hatred may be object directed, self-directed, and may be internalized through identification with hated or hating objects (Kernberg 1992a). Hatred may be rationally or irrationally mobilized and directed, and it is a universal response to threats or injuries to oneself or love objects. Individuals with the pathological affective, cognitive, and control structures associated with extreme hatred are often predisposed to the enactment of violent aggression and explosive rage. In some individuals and groups, there is a delicate love-hate balance, and a delicate balance between the intensity of rage and hate and capacities for defense, control, and regulation. Hatred may be moderated and modulated through love, but love objects and the ideals they represent may be swept aside in massive regression or in the loss of love and restraints in the sheer struggle for survival. Hate may defend against love, and love may defend against the awareness and expression of hate.

In describing erotized hate in perversions and as condition of sexual arousal, Stoller (1979) pointed to perverse dehumanizing and destructive tendencies. Bollas (1985) described "loving hate" as preserving an object tie, similar to Blum's (1981) formulation of the attachment to the ambivalently hated and loved "inconstant object" or self-object. Hatred may be adapted to or drawn into the service of other functions such as self-constancy and self-esteem regulation. Pao (1965) proposed ego syntonic uses of hatred, as in the formation of identity, though an essentially negative identity.

With its destructive potential, hatred is subject to all the defenses. Hate is repressed to protect the love object and, because of guilt, the ambivalently loved object. Hatred may be focused and intensified, mobilized and expressed through identification. Identification and indoctrination influence the aims and object of hatred in both the individual and the group. In the psychoanalytic situation, hate is perhaps more likely to disrupt or interrupt treatment than forbidden love. Love is easier to tolerate and enjoy than hate, in both the transference and countertransference. Chronic countertransference hate, inevitably registered and experienced by the patient, is a significant factor in analytic stalemates and failures. Leaving such an analytic dyad and transferring to a different analyst may be compared with leaving a regressive, sadomasochistic marriage or group.

The vicissitudes of hate in relation to conscience are as variable and complex as those of love. Instead of being regarded as a threat to the self or object, hate may be authorized

and rationalized, justified and sanctified. Because it is so destructive to familial and group cohesion, it is easily displaced
and projected outside the family or group. Given sufficient
traumatic injuries, narcissistic wounds, internal conflict, and
frustration, hate may be readily activated, amalgamated with
rage. There is also no simple relationship between hate and
rage, though they are usually bound together. A rage center is
found in the human brain near the hypothalamic locus for
sexual excitement. No such locus is known for the attitude of
hate. Hate may be present without rage, but rage is probably
associated or alloyed with some aspect of hate.

GROUP PROCESS:
SOCIAL AND CULTURAL FORCES

One of the most important factors in the release of group
aggression, hate, and violence is the feeling of justification and
altered standards of justice. Individual moral judgments are
suspended, and, in the military or mob, new standards and
values are imposed. This implies a regression and loss of
superego autonomy with greater degrees of external rather
than internal control and an alteration in the organization and
contents of the superego. The individual regression is highly
variable, depending on superego strength and stability and the
overall personality. The new identifications with the leader
and the group have all the power and prestige attributed to the
idealized leader and the collective ideal values of the group.
What was previously considered right or wrong may be
entirely reversed, and what is approved by the group is considered to be altogether right and righteous. The search for
new idealized heroes and new ideals is part of the superego
transformation of adolescence and also leads to greater dependence on the peer group and its values. Socially appropriate
college students in the Milgram (1963) experiment, when

encouraged by authorities, inflicted what they thought were injurious electric shocks on hapless fellow subjects. The release of aggression and sadism was authorized and enacted within the experiment.

An altered sense of justification and justice was a major factor in witch hunts, religious and political violence, and the persecution of the heathen and heretics, and it culminated in its most extreme form in the Nazi quasi–holy war against the Jews. The Jews were considered a degenerate race; they were evil, cancerous; they were a disease that might infect the Aryan blood; and they were a genetic threat to the aggrandized, "pure" Aryan genotype. This racial anti-Semitism was more virulent because it was incurable by conversion or acculturation, and intermarriage was a genetic danger. The "righteousness" of the cause converged with justification and rationalization for the splitting off, externalization, and projection of everything evil and despised onto the Jews. In Nazi ideology, they were criminals, social parasites, and predators. The Jews represented everything unacceptable in the self and object world. Finally, the Jews were described as subhuman, and this categorization was used to preclude empathy and to rationalize the "final solution." The Jews were deserving of genocide and destined for extermination. Referring to this type of splitting, Freud (1930) observed, "In this respect the Jewish people have rendered most useful services to the civilizations of the countries that have been their hosts; but unfortunately, all the massacres of the Jews in the Middle Ages did not suffice to make that period more peaceful" (p. 114). They were a ready, stereotyped, historical scapegoat, an easy target for the aggression of and punishment by the majority.

Righteous wrath and mass paranoia were important factors contributing to the horrors of the Holocaust and the monstrosity of limitless mass murder. Hatred and violence against a designated, "dangerous" group that was so devalued as to be dehumanized were considered to be appropriate. The release of pent-up rage and hate was promoted and rewarded. Even war had rules and conventions, but these rules did not apply to the condemned group. An enemy was necessary, and though allies were sought, betrayal was feared. It was not enough to conquer or subdue, but rather to totally annihilate the enemy. There was no reprieve for noncombatant civilian "subhumans," and no likelihood of survival through submission or surrender. New rules and values granted permission for mayhem and murder toward the defined "enemy" group. The mass paranoid splitting and projection fostered fears of retaliation and revenge. This contributed to genocide, so there would be no survivors who could bear children or bear witness, or become avengers.

The simultaneous operation of different systems of injunctions and ideals, inside and outside the group, suggests contradiction and polarization more than inconsistency or disharmony. The superego is "split," and there are, metaphorically, multiple superegos. The superego cannot only be bribed or tricked, corrupted and seduced, but also suspended and seemingly replaced. Like the external police, the superego "may not be around when needed most" (Arlow 1982). Power may be admired and "getting away with murder" condoned. There can be a uniform code of injustice. It may only take basic training and military indoctrination to acquire a military superego that temporarily permits killing and destruction.

Sexual behavior, as well, may be rapidly deregulated, sometimes beyond what was intended. Sexual mores may also be suspended. Masters and Johnson (1966) did not require prostitutes for their sexual research. Hospital staff volunteers, under the aegis of medical science and research, readily participated in laboratory studies. Sex acts were performed in the presence of the experimenters and on camera. Some members of the medical staff described their laboratory responses as more exciting than marital sex at home. They presumably had the permission of the medical authorities and could concurrently abrogate or defy their usual standards and values. There is conclusive evidence that the superego is never fully autonomous and is suspended or submerged with introjection of new external authority. Standards and values that were once cherished can be brushed aside with ego justification and rationalization. The superego can be altered by illness, brain injury, drugs, alcohol, groups, and social sanction. Moral judgment remains relative, contextual, and subjective. Analysts and their institutions are also vulnerable to the compromise of integrity (Rangell 1974), for example, by using unethical means for alleged lofty ends or corrupted by power and powerful colleagues and patients.

REGULATION, COUNTERAGGRESSION, AND SELF-DEFENSE

In the aftermath of Hiroshima and in the age of the dissemination of nuclear weapons, the possibility of an atomic attack by terrorists, a nuclear holocaust, cannot be dismissed. It is, therefore, all the more important to consider how to achieve regulation of aggression and violence. When is external aggression not simply rationalized, but rational and justified? Are there not righteous or necessary wars? If the Nazis had succeeded, who knows what other groups might have been destined for dehumanization and extermination and whether civilization could have survived. The Nazis intended that after the genocide of the Jews, the Slavic races were to be permanently subdued and to become their slaves. Intellectuals and dissidents in the slave groups were to be exterminated so as to perfect a slave mentality that would easily be subjugated by the master Aryan race. There are no easy answers to such questions as when it is necessary to meet violence with violence, and when group or national aggression may prove to be adaptive and constructive.

What is difficult to decide is under what circumstances it is appropriate to aggressively resist tyranny and injustice. To fight aggression may seem desirable or necessary, but the use of force instead of moral suasion, the resort to violent defiance of unjust laws, and the seduction of violence that may then follow are not without ambiguity and inner conflict. Moral judgments are only self-evident, if ever, at the extremes of clearly defined good and evil, where there are no shades of gray. Otherwise, moral and ethical dilemmas abound. Total-itarian regimes corrupt superego standards and values while limiting personal responsibility and threatening personal safety. Are those who were only silent or who passively conformed to official oppression and persecution craven or "scared stiff," realists or opportunists vicariously gratified or mortified?

Regulated aggression is essential for development and personal survival, and its reappearance in children is associated with recovery from illness and trauma. Individual self-defense and adaptive aggression may be absolutely necessary for safety and survival. However, the answer to the wide-spread problems of anomalous delinquency and crime, gang violence and predatory behavior can hardly be only through counterattack and police action.

Some of the most primitive aspects of the talion principle operate in the individual psyche, as mediated through the group. The harsh and punitive dimensions of the superego are reinforced, and the individual and the group can expect that their violence will incur retaliation or self-directed aggression (Blum 1985). Violence is not only contagious, it begets new, punitive, and vengeful violence. Violence is unconsciously seductive, sweeping away restraints and inhibitions. Violence becomes a breeding ground for fantasies of rape and plunder as well as retaliation and acts of revenge. It is difficult for an individual confronted by aggression in an atmosphere of violence to remain calm and cool. But this buys time for reason, reflection, and restraint. It is a measure of superego autonomy to not succumb to superego regression with a loss of mature moral judgment and values.

With the advent of modern long-range high-technology weaponry, the enemy remains nameless and faceless and is easily dehumanized. Considerations of morality and guilt are more readily suspended. The enemy is an unknown stranger, who does not impinge upon one's sense of self or fit into one's group. It is questionable whether the stranger anxiety sometimes seen in infants in the eighth month of life is developmentally related to "strangers" of later life, those who are transformed into strangers, and alien groups. The development and decline of infant stranger anxiety has been related to the advance in object relations and diminished omnipotence (Spitz 1965). The hostility to strangers in adult life is regressive and projects hostility away from self and love objects and often onto a socially sanctioned scapegoat. Such adult anxiety and hostility has a far more complex development and structure, and the superego evolves long after infantile stranger anxiety has subsided.

Greater psychological distance, psychological alienation, and dehumanization of the enemy facilitates socially sanctioned mayhem and murder. This is more likely to be directed against relatively defenseless minority and "out" groups from which the majority may more readily feel estranged. The initially diminished danger of retaliation may be associated with an invitation to circular violence that feeds on itself. Similar dynamics are found in social and racial bias, although prejudice is not inevitably enacted in violence.

The usual precepts of the superego that inhibit aggression and restrain violence against the self and others are more likely to undergo more alteration in traumatized individuals. Regressive deregulation tends to be accompanied by deneutralization, that is, a loss of tamed and controlled aggression and the reappearance of unneutralized aggression (Hartmann 1955).

The subcultures of the alienated and the homeless, so vulnerable to manipulation by charismatic, grandiose, paranoid psychopaths, are a festering sore, fertile for untamed outbursts of destructive aggression and violence. People who have been humiliated, oppressed, and persecuted have always had a stake in rebellion and a motive for violent protest. The potential for nearly obligatory, aggressive acting out may be found in all traumatized individuals. There are residues of internalized panic and rage, and trauma leaves a vulnerability to regression and repetition that may be mobilized and externally exploited. The traumatized individual is likely to show intensified sadomasochism and an unconscious and automatic identification with the aggressor. Identification with the aggressor and frustrater is part of superego development. But with trauma, identification with the aggressor, and the accompanying fantasy role reversal of aggressor and victim, function to overcome traumatic helplessness and anxiety. Such identification may also serve aggrandizement and revenge, and defend against feelings of impotent hate, rage, and victimization.

Identification with the victim, the protector, and the comforter contributes to empathic concern and sympathetic interest. The capacity for empathy for, and trial identification with, the injured and the needy may be fundamental to superego formation and to the later emergence of feelings of remorse and penance. That the foe is nameless and faceless, attacked at a distance, makes the transition from friend to foe more readily accomplished in the formation of a paranoid-type system. Ego distance and detachment undermine trial identification with the injured foe. Empathy and sympathy, pity and remorse are more likely to be absent when battles are fought with a great physical and psychological distance between the adversaries. The geographics are, however, only a superficial factor compared with intrapsychic alienation from and animosity toward objects in the immediate surround, and the "enemy within" of self-loathing. Remorse depends on the awareness of having harmed another person to whom one is able to relate and who is valued. Inconsistent or contradictory identifications may lead to great functional variability in, and vulnerability to, superego regression and alteration. Formerly sacrosanct prohibitions and admonitions may be overthrown as a fantasy of identification with the aggressor or a sadomasochistic beating fantasy is enacted.

DEVELOPMENTAL CONSIDERATIONS

Severely and multiply traumatized children are often traumatized during different phases of development, over long periods of time. Some children have experienced repetitive object loss or a chaotic childhood. Some have experienced parental abuse and neglect, or protracted and multiple illnesses in themselves and/or their parents. Rapists have often been sexually abused children. Terrorists often have a history of severe childhood illness with protracted pain, restricted mobility, and solitary confinement. Such individuals are more likely to have not only violent fantasies but also propensities for violent behavior. The illness precludes appropriate regulation and release of aggression, and caregivers may misunderstand the child's irrational responses, as well as the return of activity and aggression coincident with recovery. The child's fantasies about the illness, for example, as punishment and experience of punitive or persecutory objects, will influence further superego development. Identification with the comforter, protector, and rescuer, so significant in recovery from trauma, depends upon the quality and consistency of the caregiving relationship (Blum 1987). Paranoia does not require a history of childhood persecution, but paranoia is more likely to occur when paranoid tendencies are validated by life experience. In all these situations, the usual inconsistencies, imbalances, and contradictions within the range of superego expectations are enormously magnified. The balance between the benevolent and protective superego (the good cop) and the sadistic, punitive superego (the cruel tyrant) is tipped toward absolute, punitive authority.

This balance between punitive and protective superego functions is very much dependent on qualities inherent in psychic structure and object relations. I believe that it is inaccurate to describe the archaic superego simply as harsh and punitive. The most primordial superego internalization depends upon attachment to a love object. The shadings of right and wrong are not yet present in infancy, and complex moral judgments are not possible. But at the same time, loving and guiding aspects of the parents are internalized as the child learns rules and regulations, not only to avoid disapproval but also to maintain the parental love and approval (Schafer 1960). Without a positive primary object relationship internalization remains insecure, and superego as well as ego deformation is likely to occur. Object love, more than fear of disapproval, fuels superego development. The psychopath, for example, is likely to have extremely shallow object relations and to be governed by narcissistic entitlement rather than reliable and benevolent superego regulation. The projection of aggressive impulses of the child is prominent and probably inevitable in the formation of a controlling and appropriately permitting and prohibiting superego, but the internalization of rules and regulations required for mature superego functioning will not occur without the internalization of the loving parent (good object) and that parent's authoritative, controlling attitude and ideals. In turn, excessive and uncontrolled aggression interfere with psychic structure formation, object constancy, and the integration of idealized and denigrated objects (Neubauer 1993).

Rather than an absence of superego or global developmental failure, it would, in the organized personality, be more appropriate to consider regression and areas of developmental deviation or deficit. The psychopath or sociopath descriptively lacks manifest guilt and remorse, but there may be an unconscious sense of guilt and need for punishment. The pangs of conscience are outside of awareness, but the superego may be punitive and persecutory, with a deficiency of benevolence and with defective and deviant internal regulation. Aggression, sadomasochism, punishment, and retaliation may be almost inseparably amalgamated. Violent demagogues and fanatic ideologues who invite and incite destructive social behavior also have frequently arranged their own self-destruction. The contagious excitement of violence is fortified and justified through the permission and promotion of the violence, often by identification with acting-out authorities who may derive vicarious gratification through such aggressive behavior.

Although aggression has external referents and triggers in frustration, injury, and pain, it is part of our innate reactions and drive endowment. Differentiated from assertion, external, destructive aggression is seen in the biting, screaming, thrashing child. Rage reactions are among the earliest manifestations of destructive aggression (Parens 1979). The infant without a reciprocal love object may withdraw in anaclitic depression or with relatively lesser disturbance may engage in the self-directed aggression of head-banging or self-biting and self-scratching. An understanding and sensitive caregiver helps the infant to tame and regulate affects. If the infant has an excessive predisposition to anxiety or aggression or difficulty in regulating affects, or has an unreliable caregiver, the infant may be readily overstimulated and overwhelmed. Such problems in either member of the dyad may lead to excessive, aggressive tendencies as well as difficulties in the control and mastery of aggression.

The child, only gradually and with very great struggle, internalizes parental injunctions and expects of himself control of impulses, affects, and bodily urges. Emerging during the rapprochement phase of separation–individuation, the prohibition and expectations of the caregivers may mobilize persistent hate, anger, and rageful reactions. The rage and power struggle that ensue may frighten both parent and child and may activate fears of abandonment and loss of the object's love. It is only with repeated experiences of regulated, consistent parents that the child can experience aggression without fear of retaliation and associated defenses. The toddler wins love by accepting parental injunctions and ideals that are gradually internalized in further development. This is a slow process in which the caregiver's love, tolerance, consistency in limit setting are essential for the modulation and control of universal tendencies for rage and hate.

The taming of aggression and impulse control is a long process involving both ego and superego development. It is difficult to differentiate between certain ego and superego functions in the attainment of impulse control and standards of behavior. However, internalized self-criticism and the capacity for guilt, self-blame, and self-reproach are all essential for further superego development. As development proceeds, children inevitably go through a phase of moral absolutism where right and wrong, good and evil exist only as all or none, without shadings. Before moral judgment evolves, good and bad are evaluated in terms of parental approval and disapproval. Self-evaluation proceeds with measurement against aggrandized or idealized prohibitions and ideals that are only partially internalized. The presence and attitude of the parent remain important to the child.

Toddlers and older children inevitably show their struggles with aggression in their games and play (as well as their other behaviors, fantasies, and symptoms). They display their problems in distinguishing between fantasy and real aggression, between identification with the protector and identification with the aggressor, with blaming others, such as playmates or blaming themselves, and with circumscribed or global self-blame and self-criticism. There is a balance between the wish to please to gain and maintain the approval of the parents or surrogate authorities and the fear of external disapproval or punishment.

Children commit acts of violence against other children and property, seizing and smashing toys, throwing objects, hitting and hurting playmates and themselves. They may take the role of leader, initiating violence, or they may be influenced by the contagious aggression of others, or they may vicariously derive gratification by encouraging or instigating the aggressive enactments of others. Aggressive-like toys such as swords and rockets are commonly used by boys, although there may be a difference in the way in which aggression is mobilized and expressed by boys and girls. Children may unabashedly denigrate one another and confer scatological names. They may destroy their playmates' drawings or playthings. To be sure, aggression against property is to be preferred to attacks against people. During the process of separation–individuation and superego formation, it is necessary for toddlers to return to their parents for superego supervision, limits, and external controls. As infantile ideals and injunctions are internalized, the affect of guilt overshadows and complements the developmental earlier, externally oriented affect of shame. Gradually the toddler recognizes gradations of rule violation, such as biting mother or another person versus breaking a toy, and that different violations have different consequences (Blum and Blum 1990). Learning to not repeat the offense, to apologize and feel remorse, related to undoing and reparation, and eventually to atone develops slowly, unreliably, and in brief spurts and spasms.

Close observation of the evolution of play in toddler-hood and beyond demonstrates how often the games involve the "good guys" against the "bad guys." The evildoers must be put down, and there is a gradual growth in the under-standing of transgression and the consequences of wrongdo-ing. The internal guardian not only protects the child against aggressive and vengeful impulses, but also sees to it that the villain is vanquished. This is later seen in the adult's affinity for the murder mystery and morality play. The murderer is caught and punished, and the reader can relax. The external battle between good and evil is fought out in such games as Cops and Robbers throughout the oedipal phase, the latency phase, and beyond as the superego is consolidated.

This is an area in which play both reflects and contributes to development and internalization. Unacceptable aggression is repeatedly externalized and projected onto the "bad guys." The regulations and appropriate roles are learned over and over again, reintrojected, and internalized. Heroic battles and war games are endlessly repeated. The punishment of the bad guys and opposition to "badness" is justified and increasingly sophisticated, increasingly abstract; impersonal notions of justice and moral judgments become part of the childhood "morality" play. In wars there is some loss of differentiation and integration of principles of morality and justice. A regres-sion to simple righteous war against the "bad guys" occurs. As in child play, the demonology is based upon primitive projection and splitting rather than mature moral judgment. The morality play, so significant to superego development, may also serve regression and childish precepts and values.

With regression, the timeless struggle of good versus evil is revived. If ego regression accompanies that of the superego, there are renewed problems in differentiating the more ab-stract aspects of rules and regulations and the more abstract concepts of fairness and justice. In those individuals in whom there has been prominent identification with the aggressor, the revival of righteous punishment and righteous wrath may be particularly powerful. The guardian functions of regulation and restraint may be suspended or eclipsed as identification with the aggressor and omnipotent warlord becomes dominant in fantasy and/or in behavior. As the superego itself becomes less benevolent, there is a parallel diminution of empathy for the target of aggression and loss of remorse in the aftermath of inflicted injury. Children identify with and may act out their parents' unconscious fantasies of crime, punishment, and revenge.

These individual dangers to mature superego function are enormously intensified if there is identification with a grandiose, omnipotent parent figure and a splitting off of aggression toward a common enemy. The salvation and survival of the self are equated with the destruction of the fantasied common enemy. The whole array of primitive defenses are called into play in this type of regression. The alloying of narcissism with aggression, "malignant narcissism" (Kernberg 1992b), and the glorification of power, conquest, and territory, absorb and transcend the defenses against them. Preoedipal aggression and narcissism and later oedipal conflicts over incest, homosexuality, and the threat of violent aggression within the family may be externalized and disguised within social conflict. Turf battles and class warfare have their deeper roots in unconscious conflict and trauma, though social protest should not be reduced to unconscious conflict in a genetic fallacy.

CONCLUSION

Freud (1927) pointed to the importance of both affect and cognition, that is, love, as well as the voice of reason in the

controlled mastery of aggression and hate. It is apparent that it
is necessary to control regression so that mature thinking and
feeling can be brought to bear on major conflicts. Despite the
concern that we often share that we are fiddling while civilization burns, psychoanalysis, in conjunction with other dis-
ciplines, has much to contribute to the understanding of
aggression and violence. Otherwise, we shall remain infants
marching in the infantry, misdirected by pathologically narcissistic leaders with infantile ideals and sadistic, punitive
values and attitudes. Fortified by misinformation, propa-
ganda, and indoctrination, in the service of an idealized, just
cause, doing the right thing by following proper authority,
and integrity and responsibility are readily compromised.
With the vulnerability of the superego to such rapid regression and alteration, especially within a social process, ploughshares are turned into swords and violence into a virtue. To
reverse this process and turn the swords into ploughshares
remains one of our impossible dreams.

REFERENCES

Arlow, J. (1982). Problems of the superego concept. *Psychoanalytic Study of the Child*
37:229–244. New Haven, CT: Yale University Press.
Blum, E., and Blum, H. (1990). The development of autonomy and superego precursors.
International Journal of Psycho-Analysis 71:585–595.
Blum, H. (1981). Object inconstancy and paranoid conspiracy. *Journal of the American
Psychoanalytic Association* 29:789–813.
———— (1985). Superego formation, adolescent transformation, and the adult neurosis.
Journal of the American Psychoanalytic Association 33:887–910.
———— (1987). The role of identification in the resolution of trauma: The Anna Freud
Memorial Lecture. *Psychoanalytic Quarterly* 56:609–627.
Bollas, C. (1985). Loving hate. *The Annual of Psychoanalysis* 12/13:221–237.
Freud, S. (1915). Instincts and their vicissitudes. *Standard Edition* 14:109–140.
———— (1921). Group psychology and the analysis of the ego. *Standard Edition* 18:65–143.
———— (1927). The future of illusion. *Standard Edition* 21:1–56.
———— (1930). Civilization and its discontents. *Standard Edition* 21:57–145.

Greenson, R. (1963). Why men like war. In *On Loving, Hating, and Living Well*, ed. R. Nemiroff, A. Sugarman, and A. Robbins, pp. 123–147. New York: International Universities Press, 1992.

Hartmann, H. (1955). Notes on the theory of sublimation. *Psychoanalytic Study of the Child* 10:9–29. New York: International Universities Press.

Kernberg, O. (1992a). The psychopathology of hatred. In *Affect: Psychoanalytic Perspectives*, ed. T. Shapiro and R. Emde, pp. 209–238. New York: International Universities Press.

————— (1992b). *Aggression in Personality Disorders and Perversions*. New Haven: Yale University Press.

Masters, W., and Johnson, V. (1966). *Human Sexual Response*. Boston: Little, Brown.

Milgram, S. (1963). Behavioral study of obedience. *Journal of Abnormal & Social Psychology* 67:371–378.

Neubauer, P. (1993). Presentation, Symposium on "War and Aggression," Vienna, November, 1993.

Pao, P. (1965). The role of hatred in the ego. *Psychoanalytic Quarterly* 34:257–264.

Parens, H. (1979). *The Development of Aggression in Early Childhood*. New York: Jason Aronson.

Rangell, L. (1974). A psychoanalytic perspective leading currently to the syndrome of the compromise of integrity. *International Journal of Psycho-Analysis* 55:3–12.

Schafer, R. (1960). The loving and beloved superego in Freud's structural theory. *Psychoanalytic Study of the Child* 15:163–188. New York: International Universities Press.

Spitz, R. (1965). *The First Year of Life*. New York: International Universities Press.

Stoller, R. (1979). *Sexual Excitement*. New York: Pantheon.

3

NOTES ON PERVERSIONS OF THE SUPEREGO BY HATE

Discussion of Blum's Chapter "Sanctified Aggression, Hate, and the Alteration of Standards and Values"

Henri Parens, M.D.

Harold Blum's chapter is a richly informing exploration of the phenomenon he calls "sanctified aggression" and specifically of the dynamics and plasticity within the superego that make it possible. It is a very important consideration: How do we come to feel that our hate toward others is just, laudable, and honorable? How have we throughout the history of Western civilization come to believe it just to enslave, denigrate, despise, and destroy others, at times in masses, from long before the crusades, through the ravaging of black families in Africa by Americans, to the ignominious destruction of 6 million Jews by Nazis and their collaborators, the slaughter of 15 million Soviet countrymen by the Stalinists, the slaughter of hundreds of thousands of Communist Chinese by Nationalist Chinese, to be followed by the massacre of perhaps as many as three million Cambodians by Communist Cambodians, to the current efforts of Bosnians to "cleanse" their land of Muslims, and on and on. As Vamık Volkan, the well-known analyst and a former president of the International Society of Political Psychology, said, in January 1993, worldwide, there were over 30 intra- and international wars with their inevitable massacres.

Like many before him, Blum tries to address this question, looking particularly at what happens to the superego that allows crimes against humanity to be experienced as just, as righteous. Blum's thinking ranges widely. He speaks of the idealizations and devaluations humans experience and the cardinal influence of demagoguery on humans with variably suffering psyches. He discusses the burden of hate on the ego, the defenses needed to protect the self and emotionally invested objects against this hate the self feels by regression, denial, projection, splitting, repression, rationalization, and intellectualization with resultant feelings of justification and the alteration of moral standards. To this cluster of defenses I have added generalization, vilification, and caricaturing as complements of rationalization and intellectualization.

In the spirit of pushing Blum's inquiry further, I would like some clarification of Blum's statement that "Hatred is a complex, affective state *alloyed* with aggression that is not easy to define." Is this the problem of drive versus affect? Does he see hate as an affect and aggression as drive? I have struggled and continue to struggle with this question and I shall say more about it in a moment.

It is not clear to me if Blum is using the term *aggression* to mean only what I call hostile destructiveness, which includes hostility, rage, and hate, or if he is using the wider concept of aggression that includes hostile destructiveness and what many analysts have insisted also should be considered under the term *aggression*, namely, nondestructive aggression.

Among the theories of aggression available to us, one parameter along which they can be aggregated is just this, that some define it as destructive only; they allocate nondestructive aggression to "assertiveness," assuming these qualities to be originally unrelated forces in the human psyche. These theories include that embraced by academic psychology, most handsomely represented by Dollard et al. (1939), and by Otto Kernberg (1982, 1992) and by Stechler and Halton (1987) among analysts. Lichtenberg (1989) could be included in this group. The other theories define aggression to range from nondestructive aggression through hostile destructiveness. Among these are Freud (1915, 1930), Winnicott (1950), Waelder (1956), Lantos (1958), Spitz (1969), Greenacre (1960), Storr (1968, 1972), Solnit (1972), McDevitt (1983), and Parens (1973, 1979, 1989). It really does matter how we define aggression and it pertains not only to Blum's statement that "hate is a complex affective state alloyed with aggression" but especially to his conviction, which I share, that psychoanalysis has a significant contribution to make in offering explanations as to how the "sanctified destruction" of others arises and how it can be lessened.

The major aggression theories can also be considered from the vantage point of drive versus affect. Freud saw it as drive and viewed affects as surface manifestations of drive. Many affect theorists follow Tomkins (1962, 1991) in doing away with drive altogether and explaining aggression solely in terms of affect. Emde and Stern have adopted this view. Stechler and Halton prefer the academic psychology model, which, as I understand it, separates aggression and assertiveness and was never linked to drive nor specifically to affect theory. Lichtenberg too has offered a model to replace drive and affect theories.

Holding to drive theory, Kernberg (1982, 1992) suggests that drive is organized out of the early and continuing affective experiences in object relations. Experiences are internalized as "building blocks" constituted of self and object affective interactions. It is a very attractive theory.

I see it somewhat differently, although there are key points on which what I have proposed is consonant with what Kernberg proposes, and it is pertinent to Blum's concerns. I too hold to drive theory. But it is very clear to me—as it has been to many analysts who have addressed aggression—that the affective or emotional in experience is fully determining of how the inborn drive dispositions develop. In 1915 Freud said that the drives are plastic and that experience is fully influential in their development, along the complemental series of constitution and experience.

My observational and clinical studies of aggression lead me to see affects and drives to be part of one thing in humans, not a mixture of two separate entities. The quality of what we experience affects constitutional tendencies in us that I see as libido and aggression. Hate is on the spectrum of hostile destructive affects that constitute the hostile destructive current (trend) in aggression (Parens 1991). And here is how aggression becomes hate: in humans, aggression is the inborn tendency to move toward a goal, to track down, assert oneself upon (and catch) even against resistance, bring under control and gain mastery over the object (animate or inanimate) with or without its assimilation into the self. This fundamental inherent tendency or aim in aggression can be modified (plasticity) by a key experiential factor that activates an inborn adaptive mechanism.

Unpleasure triggers or activates a modification in aggression (Parens 1979). In assuming unpleasure to be the lowest common denominator, I go beyond Blum's assertion that "aggression has external referents and triggers in frustration, injury, and pain." The modification of aggression of which I speak is dependent on the degree and intensity of unpleasure experienced; this is what changes aggression into *hostile destructiveness* (HD). It is the experience of *excessive unpleasure* that activates rage, hostility, and eventually hate (Parens 1979). HD has a benign form that is *anger* generated by unpleasure that is readily tolerable to and contained by the ego (Parens 1989, 1991). It is when an experience is felt to be excessively unpleasurable that the inborn mechanism (which is reactive to stimuli) generates the modified form of aggression, namely

HD. As long as unpleasure is not felt to be excessive, the form of HD generated is anger; when the unpleasure is experienced as excessive, HD obtains the affective character of hostility, rage, or hate. All the major theories of aggression that are not based on the death instinct are in accord that excessive unpleasure is what generates HD in humans. Hate then is experience-dependent and experience-determined. I agree with McDevitt that hate is enduring. Hate, unlike rage and hostility per se, is the hostile destructive affect that, like its counterpart love of the libidinal affects, is what especially becomes attached to object and self. This is exactly what makes hate an enduring emotional state. And as Blum suggests, "hate requires sufficient ego development," and, agreeing with McDevitt again, becomes possible and emerges during rapprochement when the child begins to establish self and object as separate entities. Object permanence plays its part in stabilizing hate and love.

It seems that rage, hostility, and hate are unavoidably generated or activated in the context of the child's relationships to objects to whom he/she is attached, on whom the child is dependent. I wonder how much the continuity of the need for relatedness stabilizes the experience of hate and makes it an enduring emotional state. It is this, as Blum asserts, the hate that is felt toward libidinal objects and self, that must find an object outside of the self and libidinal dyad. By displacement and the cluster of splitting, externalization, and projection, the hate felt within is ascribed to the victim-object. "The Jews [for Nazis] represented everything unacceptable in the self and the object world." Hate is "sanctified" by the condemnation by one's own superego of the hate attached to libidinal objects.

ABOUT THE REGULATION OF HATE

Blum presents some very important hypotheses regarding the superego. First, I found much evidence in observation to support Blum's hypothesis that "it is inaccurate to describe the archaic superego [or, the infantile superego] as simply harsh and punitive." And there is, he tells us, "the simultaneous operation of different systems of injunctions and ideals, inside and outside the group." It is, he suggests, as if "there are . . . multiple superegos" in us. Given certain conditions, one superego component may "be suspended and seemingly replaced." He tells us, "It may only take basic training and military indoctrination to acquire a military superego that temporarily permits killing." There is merit to the idea of different systems of injunctions and ideals within the superego that can be activated by either internal or external experience contexts. It is a sobering thought, but I think Blum is right, that although the superego can have a measure of autonomy from external influence, our superego is never *fully* autonomous. Of course, it should not be autonomous from the ego. And there are times when it should be influenced by external authority; but clearly there are times when it is disastrous. It sets a large burden on our ego that, in truth, "moral judgment remains relative, contextual, and subjective."

For, as Blum asks, citing what might have followed had the United States not gotten into World War II: "Are there not righteous or necessary wars?" The study of aggression reveals how complex a phenomenon it is. Yes, hostile destructiveness is at times needed for the sake of survival and the survival of those we love, as well as for the safeguarding of property or of one's voting rights. There are times, as Blum says, when we must "meet violence with violence." I have struggled to understand the nature of aggression and the forms that are truly adaptive and those that are not. I agree with those investigators who recognize a vast trend in aggression that is inherently nondestructive. This trend is unequivocally in the service of adaptation, of securing one's basic needs, of solving problems, and achieving one's goals. It would be somehow gratifying to be able to say that nondestructive aggression is good for the soul and hostile destructiveness is bad. But it is not so, as Blum rightly tells us. However, I do think we can draw a line. It is when the psyche gets overloaded with HD, when hate is excessive and stable, and when it is then unavoidably attached to self and objects that HD becomes maladaptive. A cause to make this hate righteous will be sought, and, no doubt, will be found.

I assume that by "regulated aggression" Blum means that it is ego mediated. He says it "is essential for development and personal survival, and [that] its appearance in children is associated with recovery from illness and trauma." Here also, it seems to me, unclarity comes from using the generic term *aggression*. I see it this way: Nondestructive aggression is essential for development and survival. Hostile destructiveness is *not* essential for development but may be for survival, as when under attack by beast or man. What we see in children recovering from illness or trauma is much less, if at all, nondestructive aggression and mostly, if not all, hostile destructiveness. Although it was in part on the basis of finding aggressive behaviors in children recovering from nearly debilitating gastrointestinal disturbance that Solnit (1970) began to question his own prior views on aggression being inherently only destructive, viewing the recovering children's "naughty behaviors"—which we also see in abused children placed in foster care who become difficult (aggressive) after a honeymoon period—as adaptive. I would say adaptive, but also hostile destructive.

STRANGER ANXIETY, XENOPHOBIA, AND SUPEREGO DEVELOPMENT

Blum raises two issues when he says he thinks it questionable whether the stranger anxiety normally seen in infants is developmentally related to what we experience as strangers in later life, as well as the phenomenon of later transforming others into strangers and alien groups. I believe Blum is absolutely right when he assumes the stranger hostility of adult life is regressive and the result of the projection of HD. I, too, believe that adult stranger anxiety and the hostility attached thereto has a far more complex development and structure than that of normal stranger anxiety, and that the superego that is the heir of the Oedipus complex evolves long after infantile stranger anxiety has subsided.

Blum wonders if stranger anxiety and the superego are linked and what their temporal correlation might be. Stranger anxiety is not limited to the eighth month of life as Spitz's (1965) initial nomenclature might lead one to assume. Stranger anxiety more or less parallels separation anxiety; they are part of the same complex "structuring of the libidinal object," as Spitz said, or to use today's more widely known Bowlby model, the complex process of attachment.

Stranger anxiety emerges in most children to a greater or lesser degree from about 5 to 6 months of age, waxing and waning often in two major peaks, the more certain one at 8 months or so and the fairly common second one from about 18 to 22 months, continuing then but becoming less intense until libidinal object constancy sufficiently stabilizes between 30 and 36 months. Spitz's explanation for stranger anxiety as part and parcel of the structuring of the libidinal object was criticized by some who proposed that, rather than Spitz's "dubious" explanation, stranger anxiety is a manifestation of an inborn and therefore quite unavoidable xenophobia! I guess some scientists preferred to think that we all unavoidably experience a morbid fear of strangers. Putting it perhaps a bit too simply, we know that where attachment is good, the infantile stranger anxiety is much less likely to lead to an eventual xenophobia in adults than where attachment is troubled.

Given that stranger anxiety may extend to the middle of year three, its time relation to the development of the superego is such that the two indeed do overlap during the superego's preoedipal formation. Following on ideas Freud wrote about in 1913 and 1926 but did not integrate sufficiently into his thoughts on superego formation, I proposed a model for a major contribution to superego formation coming from the child's normal conflicts of ambivalence (Parens 1990). I inferred from observational research that the Oedipus complex contains the child's second major conflict of ambivalence. The first conflict of ambivalence arose especially during the practicing subphase when we saw in our subjects the emergence of very taxing battles of wills with their mothers, which also peaked again during the rapprochement subphase. I am following on a challenge posed to us by Selma Kramer (1994) that we reconsider the entire question of superego formation in both the male and the female.

In view of Blum's inquiry into making the object a stranger to hate and conscience formation, we observed evidence of the internalization of maternal dictates from the end of the first year of life on, just as Spitz (1965) did. These beginnings of conscience are superego precursors. But as soon as hostile destructive feelings toward the object of attachment become clearly enough perceived by the ego, an internal conflict is felt. When can we begin to consider there to be ambivalence? When can we assume guilt to be experienced? When can we consider the beginning of the structuring of a superego? Freud's first description of superego formation can be found in *Totem and Taboo* (1913), in which he said that after the band of brothers destroyed the father, the love they felt for him surfaced, and with it, a feeling of remorse set in.

With this reasoning, and given the defenses we saw our 1-year-olds employ to cope with the HD they felt toward their mothers, including especially displacement, Blum's inquiry surely adds to our understanding of the issue under scrutiny. We saw emerging anxiety and, we assume, conflict in just 1-year-olds arising from HD feelings they initially showed toward their mothers, which led the child to displace onto a stranger or lesser cathected object that same HD the child felt toward the object of attachment. I wonder if the fledgling superego yields to the ego's defense of displacement and accepts comfortably the injunction "Thou shalt love thy mother and thy father; and find a good substitute object for the displacement of the HD you feel toward them."

CONCLUSION

We do find as Blum says, that "before moral judgment evolves, good and bad are evaluated in terms first of parental approval and disapproval." And that "As development proceeds, children inevitably go through a phase of moral absolutism where right and wrong, good and evil exist only as all or none without shadings."

Blum is absolutely right that "The usual precepts of the superego which inhibit aggression [HD] and restrain violence against self and others are more likely to undergo more alteration in traumatized individuals." Aggression theorists and clinicians have written that traumatization, by virtue of the excessive unpleasure experiences trauma causes, intensifies the generation of HD in people. Like Mahler, Kernberg, and others, I believe that the ego's intolerance of intense ambivalence leads to splitting of self and object representations. The burden of hate is greater; its discharge gains priority and may even become obligatory. All the defenses Blum listed may be activated in the service of this discharge. Traumatization thus may greatly facilitate the path to scapegoating and prejudice.

I agree with Blum's caution that although "Turf battles and class warfare [may] have their deeper roots in unconscious conflict and trauma, . . . social protest should not be reduced to unconscious conflict." That is, we should not explain these on such a basis. It is especially to Blum's note that "Psychoanalysis . . . has much to contribute to the understanding of aggression and violence," that I want to say that we know enough now, from our clinical work and our research, to go beyond just understanding to the prevention of excessive hate, prejudice, and "sanctified" violence.

REFERENCES

Dollard, J., Doob, L. W., Miller, N. E., et al. (1939). *Frustration and Aggression*. New Haven: Yale University Press.

Freud, S. (1913). Totem and taboo. *Standard Edition* 13:1–162.

_____ (1915). Instincts and their vicissitudes. *Standard Edition* 14:111–140.

_____ (1926). Inhibitions, symptoms and anxiety. *Standard Edition* 20:77–174.

_____ (1930). Civilization and its discontents. *Standard Edition* 21:59–145.

Greenacre, P. (1960). Considerations regarding the parent-infant relationship. *International Journal of Psycho-Analysis* 41:571–584.

Kernberg, O. F. (1982). Self, ego, affects and drives. *Journal of the American Psychoanalytic Association* 30:893–917.

_____ (1992). *Aggression in Personality Disorders and Perversions*. New Haven: Yale University Press.

Kramer, S. (1994). *Incest and superego*. Presented to the Philadelphia Psychoanalytic Society, Philadelphia, March 16.

Lantos, B. (1958). The two genetic derivations of aggression with reference to sublimation and neutralization. *International Journal of Psycho-Analysis* 39:116–120.

Lichtenberg, J. D. (1989). *Psychoanalysis and Motivation*. Hillsdale, NJ: Analytic Press.

McDevitt, J. B. (1983). The emergence of hostile aggression and its defensive and adaptive modifications during the separation–individuation process. *Journal of the American Psychoanalytic Association* 31:273–300.

Parens, H. (1973). Aggression: a reconsideration. *Journal of the American Psychoanalytic Association* 21:34–60.

_____ (1979). *The Development of Aggression in Early Childhood*. New York: Jason Aronson.

_____ (1989). Toward an epigenesis of aggression in early childhood. In *The Course of Life: Vol. 2, Early Childhood*, ed. S. I. Greenspan and G. H. Pollock, 2nd ed., pp. 689–721. New York: International Universities Press.

_____ (1990). On the girl's psychosexual development: reconsiderations suggested from direct observation. *Journal of the American Psychoanalytic Association* 38:743–772.

_____ (1991). A view of the development of hostility in early life. *Journal of the American Psychoanalytic Association* 39:75–108.

Solnit, A. J. (1970). A study of object loss in infancy. *Psychoanalytic Study of the Child* 25:257–272. New York: International Universities Press.

_____ (1972). Aggression: a view of theory building in psychoanalysis. *Journal of the American Psychoanalytic Association* 20:435–450.

Spitz, R. A. (1965). *The First Year of Life*. New York: International Universities Press.

_____ (1969). Aggression and adaptation. *Journal of Nervous and Mental Diseases* 149:81–90.

Stechler, G., and Halton, A. (1987). The emergence of assertion and aggression during infancy: a psychoanalytic systems approach. *Journal of the American Psychoanalytic Association* 35:821–838.

Storr, A. (1968). *Human Aggression*. New York: Atheneum.

_____ (1972). *Human Destructiveness*. New York: Basic Books.

Tomkins, S. S. (1962). *Affect, Imagery, Consciousness, Vol. 1: The Positive Affects*. New York: Springer, 1992.

_____ (1991). *Affect, Imagery, Consciousness, Vol. 3: The Negative Affects, Anger and Fear*. New York: Springer.

Waelder, R. (1956). Critical discussion of the concept of an instinct of destruction. *Bulletin of the Philadelphia Association for Psychoanalysis* 6:97–109.

Winnicott, D. W. (1950). Aggression in relation to emotional development. In *Collected Papers*, pp. 204–218. New York: Basic Books, 1975.

4

HATRED AS A CORE AFFECT OF AGGRESSION

Otto F. Kernberg, M.D.

There is little doubt today regarding the prevalence of aggression in the behavior, fantasy, and psychodynamics in patients with severe personality disorders. What does continue to trouble clinicians, theoreticians, and researchers in this field is the extent to which aggression is inborn—an instinct or a drive—and the extent to which it is secondary to frustration and trauma; in short, is aggression the result of early experience or of constitution and genetics?

THEORETICAL CONSIDERATIONS

Studies of the history of patients with severe personality disorders and of children at high risk for psychopathology has shown growing evidence that early exposure to violence and to physical, psychological, and sexual abuse, particularly incest, are significantly more frequent in the background of these patients than in milder personality disorders and the population at large (Paris 1993). At the same time, evidence is also increasing that abnormality of neurochemical and neurohormonal systems may be related to significant aspects of personality pathology, particularly proneness to aggressive and reckless behavior, pointing to the importance of genetic and constitutional determinants of what is somewhat loosely called "temperament" (Stone 1993)—the inborn disposition to a certain level of intensity, rhythm, and threshold for affective response. Temperament also includes genetically and constitutionally determined behavioral and cognitive patterns, such as some gender-specific traits. Accepting in theory the possibility that both genetic and constitutional factors and environmental and psychodynamic factors may play roles, the question remains how to conceptualize aggression and understand its involvement in the development of severe psychopathology.

Contemporary biological instinct theory has evolved into an integrated view of the role of instinct and environment in conceptualizing inborn dispositions to behavior patterns that are activated under determinate environmental conditions, leading to a sequence of activation of exploratory and consummatory behaviors under the influence of environmental factors in average, expectable environmental conditions. This chain of events leads to the overall organization of behavioral sequences that we designate as instinct; inborn behavior dispositions and environmental triggers jointly constitute, therefore, the structural elements of instinctive behavior.

This conception of instincts in biology may be applied to psychoanalytic theory and lead to a concept of drives as combined instinctive and environmental motivational systems, specifically, libido and aggression (Kernberg 1992). Behind the distinction between the concepts of drive and instinct lies Freud's corresponding differentiation—unfortunately obscured by the *Standard Edition*'s translation—of

Instinkt and *Trieb*. In fact Freud distinguished between biological instincts as behaviors typical for a species, inborn, stable, and invariant, common to all the individuals of that species, and what he designated as drives, that is, highly individualized, developmentally consolidated motivations that emerge between the body and the mind and constitute the unconscious determinants of psychic life that reveal themselves in mental representations and affects (Holder 1970).

Affects are instinctive components of human behavior, that is, inborn dispositions that are common to all individuals of the human species (Kernberg 1992). They emerge in the earliest stages of development and are gradually organized, as part of early object relations, into gratifying, rewarding, pleasurable affects or libido as an overarching drive, and painful, aversive, negative affects that, in turn, are organized into aggression as an overarching drive. Within this conceptualization, affects are the inborn, constitutionally and genetically determined modes of reaction that are triggered first by various physiological and bodily experiences, and then by the development of object relations from the beginning of life on.

Rage, within this conceptualization, represents the basic affect of aggression as a drive, and the vicissitudes of rage explain, in my view, the origins of hatred and envy as well as of anger and irritability as moods. Similarly, the affect of sexual excitement constitutes the core affect of libido, which slowly and gradually evolves out of the primitive affect of elation. Elation is produced by the infant's early sensual responses to intimate bodily contact with mother.

Unlike Fairbairn (1954) and Kohut (1971), who conceptualized aggression as secondary to frustration of the need for love, I believe the capacity for both love and hatred is inborn and that both require the environment (objects, *au fond*) to be activated and developed. The most severe cases of borderline personality organization give evidence of a severe primary inhibition of the sexual response derived from lack of sufficient activation of bodily sensuality and an overriding development of aggressive reactions in the context of major disturbances in early object relations, particularly of the mother–infant dyad.

Krause (1988) has proposed that affects constitute a phylogenetically recent biological system evolved in mammals to signal the infant's needs to its mother, corresponding to a parallel inborn mother's capacity to read and respond to the infant's affective signals, thus protecting the early development of the dependent infant mammal. This instinctive system reaches increasing complexity and dominance in controlling the social behavior of higher mammals, particularly primates, and culminates in the psychological development of affects in the human being. Affectively driven development of object relations, in other words real and fantasied interpersonal interactions that are internalized as a complex world of self and object representations in the context of affective interactions (Kernberg 1980), constitute the determinants of unconscious mental life and of the structure of the psychic apparatus. Units of a self representation, an object representation, and a dominant affect linking them are its building blocks. Affects are integrated into unconscious drives, and libido and aggression as overall supraordinate drives are represented, in turn, in each enacted internalized object relation by the affect characteristic of that object relationship. Affects, in short, are both the building blocks of the drives and also serve as signals of the activation of drives in the context of particular internalized object relations.

This theoretical formulation helps to clarify some apparent differences in the development and organization of libido and aggression as drives. The affect of elation—maximized under conditions of both gratification of the baby at the breast and with intimate bodily contacts, particularly those involving specialized sensuous zones—activates, fosters, and structuralizes the development of sexual excitement in all its pregenital and genital aspects. Out of primitive elation evolves the specific and core affect of sexual excitement, as well as the affective aspects of longing, tenderness, and concern.

By the same token, aggression as a drive develops out of the primitive crying response that evolves into the affect of rage first, and into the crying response as part of sadness later. Hatred, the core affect of aggression as a drive, is a later, structuralized aspect of rage, as is envy, a particular structural development of hatred.

The proposed theoretical reformulation of the relationship between affects and drives in psychoanalytic theory permits conceptualizing the constitutionally given and genetically determined disposition to intense activation of aggression expressed by means of temperament, that is, the inborn disposition to intensity, rhythm, and thresholds of aggressive affect activation. In this connection, cognitive deficits, minimal brain dysfunctions that interfere with the organization of perceptive stimuli and facilitate the activation of anxiety under conditions of uncertainty also may contribute to pathological affect activation. A limited capacity for time appraisal and spatial organization, for example, would increase an infant's sensitivity to separation from mother. Most importantly, traumatic experiences, such as intense and chronic pain, physical and sexual abuse, as well as severe pathology in early object relations would operate through the activation of aggressive affects determining the predominance of overall aggression over libidinal striving, resulting in conditions of severe psychopathology. In short, the artificial separation of nature versus nurture can be reconciled by a concept of drives that considers their constituent affect dispositions as their structural underpinnings.

Libidinal development in the infant–mother relationship presupposes the infant's innate disposition to attachment, which requires an external stimulation to become activated;

the same reasoning may be applied to the development of rage and angry protest when external circumstances frustrate the infant's needs or desires (Kernberg 1992). In both cases an internal disposition to a peak affect response is actualized by environmental stimuli—the caregiving object. At the center of each of these basic responses, of a loving response to a gratifying environment and an angry response to a frustrating environment, are primitive affects.

I assume that from the onset of object relations the experience of the self relating to an object during intense affect states generates an intrapsychic world of affectively invested object relations of a gratifying and an aversive quality. The basic psychic experiences that will constitute the dynamic unconscious are dyadic relations between self representation and object representation in the context of extreme elation or rage. Symbiotic states of mind, that is, experiences of elation within which an unconscious fantasy of union or fusion between the self and object crystallize, are easily associated with the psychic implications of the baby satisfied at the breast, the elation of the baby in visual contact with mother's smiling face. That states of intense rage also imply an experience of fusion between self and object under the control of such an intense aversive affect is a conclusion derived from the transference analysis of patients suffering from severe psychopathology characterized by intense aggression.

Primitive affects are primary motivational systems that provide an integrative cognitive view of the total world of momentary experience in terms of the rewarding or aversive nature of that experience, with the implication of a desire to get closer to the source of pleasure or to escape from or destroy the source of unpleasure. Affects always include a cognitive component, a subjective experience of a highly pleasurable or unpleasurable nature, neurovegetative discharge phenomena, psychomotor activation, and, crucially, a distinctive pattern of facial expression that serves a communicative function for the caregiver. From this viewpoint, affects as a primary communicative system, serve, in Krause's (1988) terms, a basic biological function that supersedes more primitive physiological regulating systems. An inborn capability to "read" the affective implications of facial expression of the caregiver completes the infant's primitive system of communication basic to attachment in the behavioral realm, and to building up an internalized world of object relation in the intrapsychic realm.

The inborn capacity to "read" the affect expressed in the mother's face complements the infant's inborn capacity for specific facial motor patterns expressing his varying affect states. This early communicative system has a crucial role in the organization of early affects. As Krause has shown, a discrepancy between the infant's subjective experience and mother's affective expression may lead to a lack of organization of early affect patterns, or their disorganization, which, starting out as an expression of a mother's lack of attunement with her own or the infant's subjective state or behavior ends up with the infant's incapacity to integrate his own subjective experience and affective expression, further disturbing the nature of early object relations.

In short, early affect activation initiates the infant's object relation with mother; the nature of this object relationship may further contribute to organizing or disorganizing the affect, and early disorganization of affect states may in turn result in profound and early distortions of internalized object relations. Krause has demonstrated such disorganization of affect states, for example, in the facial expression of affect states in schizophrenic patients, and in the affective implications of stuttering.

Anger and rage, aversion and disgust, contempt and resentment are affects integrated into and serving to express particular aspects of aggression as an overall, hierarchically supraordinate drive. If we accept a modified version of

Mahler's developmental schemata (Mahler et al. 1975), that very early differentiation taking place during low-level affect states alternates with states of mind that reflect the development of the symbiotic phase under conditions of peak affect states, then Mahler's contributions to the understanding of normal and pathological symbiosis fit comfortably with the view I am proposing of early development. In my view, ego maturation and development under conditions of low-level affect states and the gradual construction of the dynamic unconscious during peak affect states permits us to integrate infant observation with our growing understanding of the structural characteristics of the dynamic unconscious derived from psychoanalytic exploration.

Aggressively invested undifferentiated self and object representations, built up separately from libidinally invested undifferentiated self and object representations, characterize the basic layer of the dynamic unconscious and reflect early symbiosis. The subsequent differentiation of self and object representations within both the libidinal and aggressive domains establishes the structural characteristics of separation-individuation and the psychopathology of borderline personality organization. I believe there is an indissoluble connection between internalization of early object relations and affect states, an indissoluble unit of the self-representation/object-representation dyad and the affective context of this dyad.

Drive neutralization, according to this concept, implies the integration of libidinally and aggressively invested, originally split idealized and persecutory internalized object relations, leading to an integrated concept of the self, an integrated concept of significant others, and the integration of derivative affect states from the aggressive and libidinal series into the toned-down, discrete, elaborated, and complex affect disposition of the phase of object constancy.

PSYCHOPATHOLOGY

Under certain conditions the aggressive drive dominates the early development of the psychic apparatus so powerfully that it leads to the psychopathological structures that we observe in psychosis, borderline personality organization, the severe types of perversion, and some psychosomatic disorders. The most central clinical observation in such conditions from a psychoanalytic viewpoint is the activation of intense, pervasive rage in the transference. From mild, chronic irritation and irritability to acutely focused and intense expression of anger, the patient easily shifts into the basic affect of rage, which, when its unconscious fantasy elements are explored, eventually reveals the structural characteristics of hatred.

The earliest function of rage is the effort to eliminate a source of irritation or pain. Rage is thus always secondary to frustration or pain, although the intensity of the rage response may depend upon temperamental features. A second function of rage is to eliminate an obstacle or barrier toward gratification. Here the dynamics are more complex: an obstacle has to be eliminated to reach a fantasied or real source of gratification. This is the prototype for a third, higher developmental level function of rage, namely the elimination of a bad object, that is, a supposedly willful source of frustration standing between the self and the gratification of a need.

Klein (1940, 1946) postulated the immediate transformation of very early states of severe frustration, the absence of mother, into the fantasied image of a bad mother, the original bad inner and external object. I agree with Laplanche (1992), however, that later traumatic experiences may retrospectively transform earlier experiences into secondarily traumatic ones and that, therefore, the point at which the rage-related internalized object relation crystallizes is not as important as the fact that it does.

At a still more advanced developmental level, the wish is no longer to destroy the bad object, but to make it suffer; here, we are definitely in the complex developmental area in which pleasure and pain combine. Sadism expresses a condensation of aggression with pleasure, and the original affect of rage appears transformed into hatred with new, stable, structural characteristics. At a further level of development, the wish to make the bad object suffer shifts into the wish to dominate and control the bad object in order to avoid fears of persecution from it; now obsessive mechanisms of control may psychopathologically regulate the suppression or repression of aggression. Finally, in sublimatory aspects of the aggressive response, the search for autonomy and self-affirmation, for freedom from external control, reflects characteristics of the original, self-affirmative implications of rage.

Hatred, I propose, is a complex, structured derivative of the affect rage that expresses several wishes: to destroy a bad object, to make it suffer, and to control it. In contrast to the acute, transitory, and disruptive quality of rage, it is a chronic, stable, usually characterologically anchored or structured affect. The object relationship framing this affect expresses concretely the desire to destroy or dominate the object. An almost unavoidable consequence of hatred is its justification as revenge against the frustrating object; the wish for revenge is typical of hatred. Paranoid fears of retaliation also are usually unavoidable accompaniments of intense hatred, so that paranoid features, a wish for revenge, and sadism go hand in hand.

One complication of hatred derives from the fact that very early frustration and gratification are experienced as stemming from the same source. Hence the obstacle to gratification is the origin of that gratification, which brings us to the psychopathology of envy. I am referring to Klein's (1957) explanation of envy as a major manifestation of human aggression. Very early frustration—in Klein's terms, the absence of the good breast—is experienced by the baby as if the breast withheld itself, with an underlying projection into the breast of the baby's aggressive reaction to that frustration. The baby's aggression takes the form of greedy wishes to incorporate. The frustrating breast is experienced as greedily withholding itself. The breast that aggressively withholds itself is, in turn, hated, and its fantasied contents are spoiled and destroyed. A vicious circle may ensue, in which the destroyed and destructive breast is experienced in a persecutory way, thus exaggerating and prolonging further the experience of frustration and rage. Here lies the origin of envy, the need to spoil and destroy the object that is also needed for survival, and, in the end, the object of love. The introjection of the image of a spoiled, destroyed breast leads to a sense of internal emptiness and destruction, which may damage the previous introjection of the good breast that was lost, so that the effects of envy and the related development of greed corrode both the good external and the good internal object.

The clinical study of patients with narcissistic personality disorder regularly reveals both unconscious and conscious envy as a major affective expression of aggression. As we move from the better-functioning narcissistic pathology to severe narcissistic personality disorders with overt borderline functioning, that is, with generalized lack of impulse control, of anxiety tolerance, and of sublimatory channeling, the intensity of aggression mounts, reaching a maximum in the syndrome of malignant narcissism. At times, the intensity of hatred is such that it results in a primitive effort of denial of hatred by means of the destruction of all awareness of the affect, a transformation of aggressive affects into action or acting out; in addition to defending against the subjective awareness of the affect, the action obliterates ordinary cognitive functioning. These developments characterize the syndrome that Bion (1957) described as constituted by arrogance, curiosity, and pseudostupidity; here, envy and hatred become almost indistinguishable.

Most patients with severe histrionic, hysteroid, or borderline personality disorder, and with severe self-destructive, self-mutilating, suicidal, and/or antisocial trends always also evince strong elements of envy within the context of intense activation of hatred. On the other hand, what might be called the "purest" manifestation of hatred—with relative absence of envy per se—may be seen in patients who have been physically traumatized and in some victims of sexual abuse or incest.

What is striking, in this context, is that the greater the envy, the more likely is an actual perception of the envied or hatefully envied person as one who possesses qualities that are highly desirable or "good." In other words, the object of hatred is experienced as an object that in some ways possesses the goodness and values that the patient misses and desires for himself. This development does not take place when pure hatred is directed at an object perceived as a dangerous, sadistic enemy. Hatred aims at the destruction of a source of frustration perceived as sadistically attacking the self; envy is a form of hatred of another perceived as sadistically or teasingly withholding something highly desirable. Typically, although not always, patients with severe narcissistic pathology have a history of a relationship with a parental figure who seemed to be operating as a good enough parent, but who had an underlying indifference toward the patient and a tendency to narcissistically exploit the patient. For example, the parent may have used the patient as a source of admiration while fostering in the patient the gratification of being an admired object.

CLINICAL APPROACH

Hatred thus emerges as the more primitive, more direct derivative of rage in response to the experience of suffering, pain, or aggression; envy emerges as a special form of hatred under conditions of a relationship in which highly desirable and teasingly withheld aspects of the object complicate the experience of rageful frustration. Clinically, the clarification of the subtle differences of these affects and their effects in the transference is a crucial aspect of the psychoanalytic and psychotherapeutic work with severe personality disorders.

The first step in such a therapeutic approach is to help the patient to become aware of the intensity of his hatred and/or envy. This, in turn, will challenge the therapist's counter-transference disposition. The therapist's capacity for emotional "holding" and cognitive "containing" of the hatred that the patient must express in action or somatization rather than tolerate as psychic experience are general capacities that converge with the therapist's creative use of his countertransference awareness. As a second therapeutic step, the patient will require not only help to acknowledge the intense, painful, and at times humiliating aspects of his hate and/or envy, but also help to acknowledge the sadistic pleasure that acting out of hatred and envy provides, and that may be one of the fundamental sources of the repetition compulsion of such behavior. And as a third step, eventually the patient will have to learn to tolerate the feelings of guilt derived from his recognition that his attack on the "bad" object is at the same time an attack on the potentially good and helpful object.

Sometimes, the patient's relentless attack on the therapist corresponds to an unconscious hope that behind the projected bad object eventually an ideal good object will emerge and defuse the situation; for the patient to recognize that his or her behavior consistently interferes with the gratification of his/her own deepest wishes is extremely difficult; the ascendance of "depressive" transferences after successful working through of antisocial and paranoid transferences is a very painful yet essential aspect of these patients' treatment (Kernberg 1992).

Envy is the most typical manifestation of aggression in the transference of narcissistic personalities, expressed as unconscious envy of the analyst experienced as a good object and in greedy incorporation of what the analyst has to offer, both leading to a sense of emptiness and frustration. Unconscious envy in the analytic situation is a significant source of the negative therapeutic reaction, more primitive and severe than unconscious guilt, which expresses more advanced superego pressures and conflicts. Unconscious envy projected onto the analyst and reintrojected into superego functions may lead to unconscious envy directed against the self.

Another consequence of the structural fixation of rage in the form of hatred is an unconscious identification with the hated object. Insofar as the internalized object relation of hatred is that of a frustrated, impoverished, pained self relating to a powerful, withholding, teasing, sadistic object, the unconscious identification with both victim and victimizer brings about an intensification of the actual relationship with the frustrating object, that is, an increased dependency in reality on the hated object in order to influence, control, punish, or transform it into a good object, and, at the same time, the unconscious tendency to repeat the relationship with the hated object with role reversals, becoming the hateful object dominating, teasing, frustrating, and mistreating another object onto which the self representation has been projected. The children described by Fraiberg (1983) and Galenson (1986) illustrate by their teasing behavior this basic mechanism of identification with the aggressor.

Physical and sexual abuse have impact on the development of the psychopathology of hatred. Trauma as the actual experience of sadistic behavior of a needed, unescapable object instantaneously shapes the rage reaction into the hatred of the sadistic object. The heightened prevalence of physical abuse, sexual abuse, and witnessing of violence in patients with severe psychopathology, including borderline personality disorder, affective disorders, dissociative disorders, post-traumatic stress disorders, antisocial personality disorders, and severe forms of eating disorders, has been reported in this country and abroad (Grossman 1986, 1991, Marziali 1992, Paris 1993, Perry and Herman 1993). Even granting the distortion of statistical analyses under the impact of the current, ideologically motivated stress on incest and sexual abuse, the evidence of such abuse as one significant etiological factor in the development of severe personality disorders is convincing. The underlying mechanism, I am suggesting, is the establishment of an internalized object relationship under the control of structured rage—that is, hatred.

When hatred overwhelmingly dominates an unconscious world of internalized object relations, primitive splitting operations persist, resulting in a borderline personality organization characterized by an internal world of idealized and persecutory object relations with a dominance of the latter and their corollary of paranoid tendencies, characterologically structured ego-syntonic hatred, sadism, and revengefulness; dissociated efforts are made to escape from a persecutory world by illusory and dissociated idealizations. Under traumatic conditions, then, the basic mechanisms would include the immediate transformation of pain into rage and rage into hatred; hatred consolidates the unconscious identification with victim and victimizer.

Let us now explore some clinical manifestations of patients dominated by hatred and the related desire to destroy the origin of their suffering as they perceive it, that is, the hated and hateful persecutory object. The most important clinical manifestation of the dominance of hatred in the transference is the patient's attributing to the therapist an intense, relentless degree of hatred. By means of projective identification, the internal world of torturer and tortured, tyrant and slave are enacted in the form of attributing to the therapist the role of sadistic tyrant, and, by means of unconscious efforts to provoke the therapist into such a role and to control him in order to limit his dangerousness, the induction of conditions in the countertransference that eventually tend to activate whatever role responsiveness the therapist possesses to fulfill the patient's fearful expectations.

Under extreme circumstances, typically seen in schizophrenic panic and rage attacks but also with transference regression in borderline patients, the patient's fear of his own hatred and of the hatred projected onto the therapist is such that reality itself becomes intolerable. If, under conditions of symbiotic regression in the transference or even intense activation of projective identification in nonsymbiotic conditions, the entire world is a sea of hatred, to block out the awareness of reality is the most primitive and dominant mechanism for dealing with this situation. Efforts to destroy the awareness of reality may lead to psychotic confusional states, or, in nonpsychotic patients, to a malignant transformation of the therapist–patient dyad in which all honest communication is suppressed, and what I have called psychopathic transferences prevail: the patient is deceptive, expects the therapist to be deceptive, all communication takes on a pseudo quality, and violent affect storms are expressed in dissociated forms.

Under less extreme conditions, such as one may see in patients with the syndrome of malignant narcissism, the patient may manifest intense curiosity about the therapist, to the extent of actively spying on the therapist's life; the patient shows consistent arrogance and contempt for the therapist, and an incapacity to conduct cognitive communication with the therapist that may amount to a form of pseudostupidity (Bion 1957). The gradual working through of such conditions in the transference may eventually give rise to the patient's tolerance of his hatred rather than having to project it (Kernberg 1992). Conscious tolerance of hatred may then be expressed as joyful attacks, insults, depreciation, and teasing of the therapist, which may be gradually traced to its origins—to traumatic situations from the past and intense envy of the therapist as an individual not controlled by the same terrifying internal world of the patient.

Another manifestation of primitive hatred that the patient cannot tolerate in conscious awareness is the transformation of hatred into somatization in the form of primitive self-mutilation; these are patients who chronically mutilate themselves—pick at their skin or mucosae—and present other patterns of primitive sadomasochistic behavior. Characterologically anchored suicidal tendencies in borderline patients are another expression of self-directed hatred.

The antisocial personality proper may be conceived as a personality structure so dominated by hatred that primitive, split-off idealizations are no longer possible; the world is populated exclusively by hated, hateful, sadistic persecutors, and to triumph in such a terrifying world can only be achieved by one's becoming a hateful persecutor as the sole alternative to destruction and suicide. Under milder conditions, unconscious identification with the hated object and its characterological translation into antisocial tendencies, cruelty, contempt, and sadism may present in many forms. A restricted, encapsulated sadistic perversion may represent one outcome of these conflicts. As Stoller (1985) pointed out, sexual excitement always includes an element of aggression and an organized perversion typically expresses the need to undo in fantasy an experienced trauma or humiliation from the past in the sexual realm.

Progressing toward less severe types of characterological forms of hatred, the drive for power and control, the sadistic implications of certain obsessive-compulsive personality structures contain this dynamic, as is true for certain personality structures with reaction formations against dependency that express the unconscious fear that all dependent relationships imply a submission to a sadistic object. Masochistic reaction formations against identification with a hateful object internalized into the superego reflect relatively less severe outcomes of these dynamics. More frequently, the internalization of a hated, sadistic object into the superego may be manifest as sadistic moralism—the tendency toward "justified indignation," and moralistic cruelty.

At a sublimatory level of transformation of hatred, self-assertion, courage, independent judgment, moral integrity, even the capacity for self-sacrifice may include, on analytic exploration, traces of the dynamics we are exploring.

SEXUAL AND PHYSICAL ABUSE

Incest as trauma has received much recent attention, and psychoanalytic exploration of its victims indeed illustrates the basic dynamic of internalization of an object relation dominated by hatred. In exploring these psychodynamics one has to keep in mind the normal role of sexual excitement in neutralizing aggression by the erotic potential of mild physical pain. The sadomasochistic component of sexual excitement permits the recruitment of aggression in the service of love, but it is a response that, when a sexual response is overwhelmed by rage and hatred, may be transformed into sexual sadomasochism in which, we might say, love is recruited in the service of aggression. In other words, sexual intercourse may become a symbolic gratification of sadomasochistic tendencies replicating, in the sexual area, the interactions I have described in relationships dominated by hatred.

Not all sexual abuse is experienced as aggressive; unconscious infantile sexuality, the excitement, gratification, and triumph resulting from breaking oedipal barriers, as well as the guilt that such triumph produces, complicate the psychological effects of sexual abuse. Nevertheless, the distortion of superego structures brought about when cross-generational, particularly parent–child, incest occurs destroys the potential for the integration of sadistic parental images into the super-ego. The conflict between sexual excitement and guilt is thus transformed into one between frail idealization and over-whelming aggression, creating a truly traumatic situation in which libidinal and aggressive strivings can no longer be differentiated. The unconscious identification with the vic-timizer and the victim may become confused, and the repeti-tion compulsion of incest victims who transform their later sexual life into a chain of traumatophilic experiences makes it often difficult to differentiate; was the patient victim or vic-timizer?

In the clinical situation, such incest victims reactivate the identification with the dyad of victim and victimizer, and unconsciously attempt to reproduce the traumatic situation in order to undo it and to recover the ideal object behind the persecutor. In addition, the repetition compulsion expresses the desire for revenge, the rationalization of hatred of the seducer, and a potential sexualization of the hatred in the form of efforts to seduce the seducer. The psychoanalytic treatment of incest victims who have had sexual experiences with former therapists sometimes repeats these experiences with uncanny clarity. Unconscious envy of the current therapist not involved in the chaotic mixture of hatred and sexuality in which the patient experiences himself/herself as hopelessly mired is another source of negative therapeutic reactions in these patients.

Recent research (Paris 1994) confirms the importance of the history of sexual abuse as a prevalent aspect of patients with borderline personality disorder as well as their tendency toward dissociative reactions. Paris also points to a relative independence of these two factors, so that a predisposition to dissociative reactions does not seem to be secondary to sexual trauma. In clinical practice, both types of problems are seen together with some frequency, even discounting the current epidemic of multiple personalities, which at least in part appear to be iatrogenically induced. Some borderline patients present dissociative reactions in the form of amnesias, depersonalization states, and even multiple personalities of which the patients are cognitively aware but that are affectively split.

What is often striking in such dissociative states is the patient's remarkable indifference to what seems to be a dramatic psychopathological phenomenon; indeed, some patients present an almost defiant affirmation of the "autonomy" of his/her split-off personalities, while refusing to consider any sense of personal responsibility for these phenomena. Often, the mutual dissociation of alternate personality states raises the question of why some apparently not incongruous personality states appear as split from each other.

In my experience, when the clinician asks how the patient's central personality, his or her sense of awareness, concern, responsibility, relates to these split-off personality states, this triggers an immediate new development in the transference. Many patients develop a paranoid reaction to such an inquiry, which evolves into a specific transference disposition in which the therapist appears as a persecutory figure and is contrasted to other persons in the patient's life, including other therapists, who are idealized as helpful, tolerant, nonquestioning, admiring, and supportive. The patient's alternate personality states take on more specific meanings in relation to such split object representations, permitting a clarification of the function of such split states in the transference. In short, approaching the patient from the position of an assumed observing, central, "categorical" self illuminates hidden splits in the transference and permits exploration of the unconscious dynamics involved in the split personality state that are obscured by the usual, apparently untroubled enactment of these split states.

The patient now may be tempted to angrily accuse the therapist of not believing the existence of his multiple personalities. The therapist's concerned and neutral stand of being interested in the patient's experience, not questioning its authenticity but at the same time evaluating the implications for the patient's central self-experience gradually permits the patient to increase his or her own self-observing function in contrast to the previous defensive denial of concern and what might be called blind enactment of dissociative states.

In the context of our exploration of the role of aggression and hatred in severe personality disorders, the approach just outlined transforms what appears to be a dreamlike, often apparently affectless dramatization into a concrete object relation in which intense rage and hatred emerge split-off from other, idealized object relations. Once the emergence of mutually split-off peak affect states in the context of split-off primitive object relations becomes evident in the transference, the interpretive integration of these developments may proceed.

This approach is in contrast to a tendency on the part of some therapists to explore the nature of each dissociated personality state while respecting its split-off condition, bypassing the defensive denial of concern over this condition— an approach that, I believe, tends to prolong unnecessarily and even may aggravate the dissociative condition itself.

When such dissociative reactions occur in the context of real or fantasied past incest or sexual abuse, a similar defensive denial of concern over the nature of the dissociative process may often be observed. Such a development is in marked contrast to cases in which, under psychoanalytic exploration, repressed memories of past sexual abuse, including incest, are uncovered, leading to a traumatic emotional reaction that colors the psychotherapeutic relationship for perhaps several months and is gradually worked through. In this latter case, characteristics of a post-traumatic stress syndrome may emerge in the psychotherapeutic relationship; the patient shows great concern for himself/herself, an intense ambivalence in relation to the abuser, and an ambivalence regarding the patient's own past and present sexuality. The elaboration of such a traumatic recovery of memory is in sharp contrast to the long-term repetitive evocation of past traumatic sexual experiences in the context of a present-day expression of hatred, disgust, and revulsion linked with the patient's sexual life in general or the gender of the traumatizing agent.

In the latter cases, particularly when traumatic sexual memories occur repeatedly in the context of dissociative ego states, the characteristic lack of concern, denial, or a dramatic indifference toward the dissociative process described earlier may also be present. In these cases the patient may insist on engaging the therapist as a "witness" or support figure in the patient's struggle against a hated and feared sexual object. In the transference, the therapist may be identified with either the abusive object or with a conspirational helper (for example, the therapist may be viewed as the "innocent bystander" mother, who, in subtle or not so subtle ways, protected an incestuous father).

Here again, the world seems to be split between those who side with the traumatizing object and those who, in contrast, support the patient's wishes for a revengeful campaign against the traumatizing object. Because of the current cultural concerns about sexual abuse, the patient's split world of object relations may be rationalized in terms of a conventional ideology that confirms and maintains the patient's condition as a victim and justifies such a permanent split in the patient's relationship to the other gender or to sexuality in general.

I have found it very helpful to ask the patient what keeps alive the hatred in the patient's life, and what the functions of such hatred are in the patient's current conflicts. When the certainty of past sexual abuse is unclear, even in the patient's mind, the patient may insistently demand confirmation from the therapist regarding the patient's suspicions of its having occurred. The therapist's stance, that the patient's experiences are real in their present quality and that the patient himself or herself eventually will be able to clarify and gain understanding and control over the internal past, often raises the same intensity of suspicion and rage in the transference as when attempting to clarify the relationship between the patient's central self experience and a dissociative state.

In other words, the patient may not be able to tolerate the therapist's concerned but neutral position that runs counter to the overriding need to divide the world into allies and enemies. The therapist's consistent interpretation of the need to maintain such split relationships in the patient's life will eventually, under optimal conditions, permit more specific focus on the enactment of a relationship between a victimizer and a victim, with frequent role reversals of this relationship in the transference. The latter permits analyzing the patient's unconscious identification with the victimizer as well as with a victim role as the major dynamic that maintains the characterologically anchored hatred.

One major positive consequence of such a therapeutic approach is the gradual liberation of the patient's life from its infiltration with unrecognized, unmetabolized hatred. The revulsion against sexuality in victims of early sexual abuse has many roots; the invasion of psychic and physical bodily boundaries is experienced as a violent attack, and the transformation of a person in a parental function into a sexual abuser is experienced as sadistic treason, in addition to disorganizing the early buildup of an integrated if primitive superego. The reprojection of early, persecutory superego precursors in the form of paranoid tendencies intensifies even further the aggressive implication of a sexual attack, and weakens the capacity for any trusting relationship.

Unconscious guilt from the activation of the patient's own sexual impulses in the context of sexual seduction and abuse increases the revulsion toward all sexuality and the temptation to reproject such guilt feelings, thus reinforcing

the patient's paranoid approach to sexual objects and reinforcing repression of the patient's world of sexual wishes,
fantasies, and experiences. If traumatized victims of concentration camps or torture have to reencounter the awareness of
their own sadistic tendencies as they discover their unconscious identification with both victim and victimizer, the
victims of sexual abuse have to reencounter a similar awareness of their own sexuality in unconscious identification with
both self and object of the traumatic experience. The treatment cannot be considered completed if such a re-encounter
of the patient's own sexuality has not been achieved. Stoller's
(1985) understanding of the nature of erotic excitement as an
early fusion of sensuous experience and unconscious identification with an aggressive object—in other words, the erotic
roots in polymorphous perverse sadomasochism—becomes
relevant in this connection. At some point, a toned-down,
tolerable sadomasochistic tendency should become available
for retranslation into a language of erotic fantasies, opening
up the polymorphous perverse component of adult genital
sexuality.

FURTHER COMMENTS ON TREATMENT

In the treatment of patients whose transferences are dominated by hatred, it is important, first of all, to establish a
rigorous, flexible, yet firm frame for the therapeutic relationship; this step controls life-threatening and treatment-
threatening acting out. The therapist has to experience himself
as safe to be able to analyze the deep regression in the transference. Setting a contract for patients who are suicidal or who
are engaged in dangerous sexual behavior or other types of
destructiveness and self-destructiveness encourages the expression of hatred in the transference rather than into the
alternative channels of somatization or acting out. As Green

(1986) has pointed out, it is extremely important to facilitate the transformation of somatization and acting out into psychic experience in the transference.

When distortion of verbal communication exists, psychopathic transferences should be resolved first, that is, deceptiveness in the communication reduced sufficiently, for the underlying paranoid tendencies in the transference to emerge more clearly and make possible their working through. The therapist should remain alert to the activation of a victim–victimizer paradigm, analyzing in the transference this dyadic relationship as it is repeated, again and again, with role reversals—that is, with the patient's unconscious identification in the transference with both victim and victimizer, as well as projecting, at different moments, these representations onto the therapist. This requires the therapist to be extremely alert to the countertransference; painful experiences of himself as victim and the temptation to act out strong aggressive countertransference reactions as victimizer may alternate.

What must be especially guarded against in the treatment of victims of abuse is the tendency to avoid the analysis of the patient's identification with the aggressor. To treat the patient consistently as victim facilitates the projection of the aggressor role outside the transference, which perpetuates an idealized transference situation dissociated from the basic dyad controlled by hatred, thus perpetuating the patient's psychopathology. To treat the patient as a responsible adult rather than a perennial victim includes the painful need for the patient to become aware of how, in reaction to the trauma, he/she identified with the persecutor.

I have found the analysis of unconscious envy as a specific manifestation of characterological hatred particularly relevant under certain clinical conditions: first, in connection with pervasive defenses against dependency and regression in the transference typical of the narcissistic personality; second, in the presence of strong negative therapeutic reactions not based on an unconscious sense of guilt; third, in cases showing an apparent dependency on and greedy incorporation of what comes from the analyst, together with a surprising inability to learn from the experience and a persistent sense of emptiness in the analytic situation; fourth, when inordinate ambition and power appear in combination with conscious and unconscious self-devaluation and depression easily triggered by lack of gratification of expectations; fifth, in the face of habitual inhibitions of creative pursuits; sixth, when unconscious conflicts around fears of humiliation and shame are combined with paranoid fears of potentially envious and persecutory attitudes from the surrounding world; and finally, when patients continue to lack the capacity to let ideas and feelings grow as a consequence of the psychoanalytic interchange, do not trust the survival of goodness in their heart, and are not able, symbolically speaking, to "mother themselves."

The tolerance of envy, its elaboration and working through as part of emotional growth, and the sense of internal richness and wealth that derives from the capacity for gratitude and appreciation of others and the enjoyment of others' success are fundamental objectives and consequences of analytic work. The resolution of conflicts around unconscious envy permits the growth of the capacity for gratitude and derived reparatory and sublimatory potential.

There are limits, I believe, in the treatment of conditions derived from the kind of hatred I have been describing. The most fundamental one, in my experience, is the deterioration or absence of superego functions that we find in antisocial personalities, a diagnostic category that has unfortunately been overextended in *DSM-III-R* and *DSM-IV*. Patients with a syndrome of malignant narcissism, that is, narcissistic personality structures with antisocial tendencies, paranoid trends, and severe forms of self-directed or other-directed ego syntonic aggression constitute presently the limit of what I believe can be reached with analytically oriented approaches.

When ego-syntonic expression of hatred translates into a sadistic enjoyment of attacks on the therapist, the importance of emotional "holding" as well as cognitive "containing" cannot be stressed enough. The therapist's consistent work with countertransference developments, often outside the treatment sessions, may become important at such times. When hatred is denied in more complex forms, such as dissociative reactions or in efforts to seduce the therapist into an enactment of hateful revenge, the interpretive approach to such developments may temporarily increase aggression in the transference, but does permit the full analysis of the involved internalized object relation. Finally, chronic sadomasochistic developments in the transference have to be explored most carefully in terms of their information and working-through value, as contrasted to a repetitive acting out that does not advance the therapeutic task, but may simply gratify and even reinforce a new channel for acting out aggression.

REFERENCES

Bion, W. R. (1957). On arrogance. In *Second Thoughts: Selected Papers on Psychoanalysis*, pp. 86–92. New York: Basic Books, 1967.

Fairbairn, W. (1954). *An Object-Relations Theory of the Personality*. New York: Basic Books.

Fraiberg, A. (1983). Pathological defenses in infancy. *Psychoanalytic Quarterly* 60:612–635.

Galenson, E. (1986). Some thoughts about infant psychopathology and aggressive development. *International Review of Psychoanalysis* 13:349–354.

Green, A. (1986). *On Private Madness*. London: Hogarth Press.

Grossman, W. (1986). Notes on masochism: a discussion of the history and development of a psychoanalytic concept—1. *Psychoanalytic Quarterly* 55:379–413.

——— (1991). Pain, aggression, fantasy, and concepts of sadomasochism. *Psychoanalytic Quarterly* 60: 22–52.

Holder, A. (1970). Instinct and drive. In *Basic Psychoanalytic Concepts of the Theory of Instincts*, vol. 3, ed. H. Nagera, pp. 19–22. New York: Basic Books.

Kernberg, O. F. (1980). *Internal World and External Reality*. New York: Jason Aronson.

——— (1992). *Aggression in Personality Disorders and Perversions*. New Haven: Yale University Press.

Klein, M. (1940). Mourning and its relation to manic-depressive states. In *Contributions to Psychoanalysis, 1921-1945*, pp. 311–338. London: Hogarth Press, 1948.

_____ (1946). Notes on some schizoid mechanisms. In *Developments in Psychoanalysis*, ed. J. Riviere, pp. 292–320. London: Hogarth Press, 1952.

_____ (1957). *Envy and Gratitude*. New York: Basic Books.

Kohut, H. (1971). *The Analysis of the Self*. New York: International Universities Press.

Krause, R. (1988). Eine Taxonomie der Affekte un ihre Anwendung auf das Verständnis der frühen Störungen. *Psychotherapie und Medizinische Psychologie* 38:77–86.

Laplanche, J. (1992). *Seduction, Translation, Drives*. London: Institute of Contemporary Arts.

Mahler, M. S., Pine, F., and Bergman, A. (1975). *The Psychological Birth of the Human Infant*. New York: Basic Books.

Marziali, E. (1992). The etiology of borderline personality disorder: developmental factors. In *Borderline Personality Disorder*, ed. J. F. Clarkin, E. Marziali, and H. Munroe-Blum, pp. 27–44. New York: Guilford.

Paris, J. (1993). *Borderline Personality Disorder*. Washington, DC: American Psychiatric Press.

_____ (1994). *Sexual abuse and dissociative processes in the etiology of borderline personality disorder*. Plenary presentation of the Conference on Borderline Personality Disorder of the New York Hospital–Cornell Medical Center, Westchester Division, June 9, 1994 (unpublished).

Perry, J. C., and Herman, J. L. (1993). Trauma and defense in the etiology of borderline personality disorder. In *Borderline Personality Disorder*, ed. J. Paris, pp. 123–139. Washington, DC: American Psychiatric Press.

Stoller, R. (1985). *Observing the Erotic Imagination*. New Haven: Yale University Press.

Stone, M. H. (1993). *Abnormalities of Personality*. New York: W. W. Norton.

5

SOME REFLECTIONS ON THE NATURE OF HATRED AND ITS EMERGENCE IN THE TREATMENT PROCESS

Discussion of Kernberg's Chapter "Hatred as a Core Affect of Aggression"

Salman Akhtar, M.D.

Otto Kernberg's chapter is a rich, complex, and multifaceted elucidation of the phenomenon of hatred, covering a vast area including the origins of hatred, its clinical manifestations, and its technical handling during treatment. Kernberg's conceptualization is broad-based, taking into account the polarities of preformation and epigenesis, brain and mind, affect and intellect, drives and experience, trauma and fantasy, and structuring of treatment and interpretation. I will, however, discuss only two aspects of his chapter: phenomenological and treatment issues involving hatred. I will not comment on developmental issues, although my comments regarding phenomenology and technique will undoubtedly be developmentally informed. I will also discuss Dr. Kernberg's views of hatred in the context of varying psychoanalytic theories of aggression and his concluding remarks regarding areas that remain unanswered. This discussion is meant to complement his chapter.

HATRED AND THE THEORIES OF
AGGRESSION

In a comprehensive and critical survey of literature on the nature and origins of aggression (Akhtar in press), I concluded that five theoretical positions exist in this realm. One extreme, pioneered by Freud in *Beyond the Pleasure Principle* (1920) and adhered to by Ferenczi, Klein, Federn, Menninger, Eissler, and Rosenfeld, holds steadfastly to the concept of death instinct and posits aggression to be a destructive outward deflection of such an instinctual substrate. The other extreme is represented by Suttie, Fairbairn, Guntrip, and Kohut, who have dissociated themselves from the instinctual basis of human motivation altogether. While their view does allow for innate[1] assertiveness, which under the influence of frustration might turn into destructiveness, it definitely rules out innate destructiveness.

Between these extremes lie three other views that reject the death instinct but adhere to the instinct theory, viewing aggression as one of the two basic instinctual drives. The first of these three views regards the aim of aggression to be variable though mainly involving destruction. It sees the infant's motility, activity, and assertion as emanating from a noninstinctual energy source to which neutralization of instinctual aggression might also contribute. This is the position of Anna Freud, Hartmann, Kris, Loewenstein, Waelder, and Brenner. The second position extends the scope of the instinctual aggression to include infantile activity, assertion, and attempts at mastery. It considers both nondestructive and destructive aggression to be fueled from the same energy source. Moreover, it emphasizes that hostile destructiveness,

---

1. The distinction between *innate* and *instinctual* is significant here since these theorists do not totally negate the former. In a different, broader context, this distinction is also exemplified in the various fundamental human motivational systems outlined by Lichtenberg (1989).

pertinent to our topic of hate, is only elicited by unpleasure. This is the position implicitly taken by Winnicott and explicitly by Parens. The third position excludes nondestructive activity from aggression and presents a view of drives different from that traditionally held. It proposes that early pleasurable and unpleasurable affects (emanating from the evocation of hard-wired potentials by neonatal object relations) gradually consolidate into the libidinal and aggressive drives that subsequently become supraordinate motivational systems. This is the position of Kernberg, whose relationship with other theorists of aggression can be summarized as follows:

> Like Hartmann, Kernberg holds a tighter view of instinctual aggression. Unlike Hartmann, he declares that drives are not external givens but evolve from affects. Like Klein, Kernberg emphasizes the role of instinctual aggression in the earliest internalizations. Unlike Klein, he discards death instinct. Like Fairbairn, Kernberg retains the importance of early object relations in the genesis of aggression. Unlike Fairbairn, he regards the underpinnings of aggression to be fundamentally instinctual in origin. Kernberg's theory, in essence, is a reconciliation of the Klein-Fairbairn schism under the influence of Hartmann's ego psychology. It, therefore, brings the three major psychoanalytic trends in the study of aggression together. [Akhtar in press]

My reason for highlighting the diverse theoretical orientations in this realm is not only to place Kernberg's formulations in their historical and conceptual context but also to raise the possibility that the five theories of aggression might yield varying notions about hatred. For instance, one theory would view hatred as an existential imperative, another as a mere evolutionary legacy, yet another as a tragic artifact, and a fourth as a building block of psyche. Perhaps such notions differ more regarding the origins and technical handling of hatred than they do about its phenomenological aspects.

PHENOMENOLOGY OF RAGE AND HATRED

Kernberg distinguishes hatred from rage, regarding the former to be a more "complex aggressive affect" (Kernberg 1992, p. 23). Rage is ontogenetically primitive; hate is a later development (Fenichel 1954, Jacobson 1953). While excessive hate might impede the acquisition of object constancy (Mahler et al 1975), some object constancy is essential for experiencing the sustained affective state of hatred (Galdston 1987). Rage is acute, hatred chronic. Rage has disruptive effects on intellect while hatred might sharpen reasoning though not without simultaneously narrowing its focus (Akhtar 1990, Shapiro 1965). While both rage and hatred involve a conscious or unconscious fantasy involving a specific self and object relation, this fantasy is submerged in rage, more available in hatred. I find Kernberg's distinctions convincing. His point about the relative stability of hatred is especially well taken. In fact, his choice of the term *hatred* over the simpler *hate* serves to underscore this point. Webster's Unabridged Dictionary describes hate as a verb, hatred as a noun. The suffix *-red* comes from the old Anglo–Saxon *raeden* for "signifying state or condition." In assigning the feature of stability to hatred, Kernberg is therefore not only descriptively astute but on solid linguistic ground as well. He also offers a superb delineation of the myriad clinical manifestations of chronic hatred. These include paranoia, somatization, characterologically anchored suicidal tendencies, and, at a higher level of organization, the drive for power and control, and moralistic cruelty.

However, Kernberg seems to contradict himself by speaking of hatred as a "derivative of rage" at one place and of "rage derived from . . . hatred" at another place in the chapter. Perhaps his intent is to indicate a dialectical relationship between the two affects, but a little more clarification would have been helpful. Moreover, there are other differences between rage and hatred (Pao 1965) that are not mentioned by Kernberg. Rage results from ego's conflict with an external object, hate from its conflict with an external and an internal object. Rage pushes for immediate action. Hatred involves interposition of ideational process resulting in suppression of immediate muscular release (cf. Stalin's wry remark, "Revenge is best eaten cold!"). Rage comes and goes with the inciting event. Hatred simmers. Rage, attempting to modify the object's frustrating behavior, focuses upon the present. Hatred "dwells on the past, thinks of revenge in the future, and is not concerned with the present" (Pao 1965, p. 258). In this way, hatred comes to be a counterpart of idealization, which, too, only in the libidinal realm, robs the present by focusing on the past (in the form of inordinate nostalgia) or the future (in the form of pathological optimism).[2]

Rage and hatred differ in still other ways. Rage has no defensive purposes. Hatred frequently serves defensive aims against fear and guilt (Jones 1929), dependent longings (Fairbairn 1940, Hill 1938), repressed grief and separation anxiety (Searles 1956, 1962), and dread of psychotic decompensation (Gabbard, in Winer 1994). Rage has little long-term adaptive purpose. Hatred, in linking past and future, establishes a sense of continuity and might contribute to a person's identity. Finally, rage unshackles the self from the object (crush it or walk away!); its aim as stated in Kernberg's chapter here is to eliminate "a source of irritation or pain." Hatred, in contrast, has an entrapping effect since

the one who hates is beset with fears and feels pulled in different directions. The hater tends to ascribe unrealistic power and importance to the object of his hate and believes it would be disastrous to offend the omnipotent and omniscient

---

2. Elsewhere (Akhtar 1991, 1994), I have described two fantasies, namely "if only" and "someday," which represent interrelated structures of idealization with deleterious effects on psychic temporality.

object. But he feels wronged by the object and "wants to get even with it." Thus he finds himself in a state of bondage. If he remains close to the object, he may betray his hatred and provoke the wrath of the object, who could crush him. On the other hand, if he attempts to avoid the hated object, he is denying himself needed libidinal supplies. Caught in a dilemma, the hater feels trapped. [Pao 1965, pp. 258–259].

Milan Kundera (1990), the renowned novelist, has summarized the situation thus: "Hate traps us by binding us too tightly to our adversary" (p. 24). Indeed, hatred might become an ego-syntonic basis of object relations much as a tormented, yet stable, tie to a frustrating object is the basis for certain masochistic characters (Berliner 1958).

This leads us into nosology and we note, with a little surprise, that borderline personalities, though given to frequent outbursts of rage, are not hateful on a sustained basis. Chronic hatred is actually seen more often in association with the "syndrome of malignant narcissism" (Kernberg 1989), paranoid personalities, and certain aggressive and sadistic antisocial characters. Besides these individuals who hate and cannot let go of their hatred, Galdston (1987) proposes three more categories: (i) those who cannot hate, (ii) those who hate but cannot become consciously aware of their hate, and (iii) those who can hate and get over hating. While he does not use this phraseology, the three categories are perhaps constituted by "as-if" (Deutsch 1942), obsessional, and relatively healthy normal personalities respectively. If this hierarchical arrangement (as-if—paranoid—neurotic—normal) is sensible, then the question is: How can we help the patient progress along this continuum?

TECHNICAL CONSIDERATIONS

Kernberg's approach to the treatment of patients with severe psychopathology of aggression, particularly intense hatred in transference, rests upon the following postulates (Kernberg 1975, 1984, 1992). The patient's hatred is based upon the activation of a specific self-object relationship. The patient hates most what he truly needs from the therapist: unwavering dedication to him. The patient also hates, because he envies it, the therapist's creativity and patience. In addition, the patient employs defenses against an awareness of his hatred, especially its pleasurable aspects. Kernberg then moves on to highlight the resonance of the patient's hatred in the analyst's subjectivity. He describes four possible countertransference reactions under such circumstances (for other outcomes of countertransference hatred, see Maltsberger and Buie 1974). The therapist might (1) emotionally withdraw from the patient; (2) view the patient as a mere victim, collude with the projection of the victimizer role to the outside of transference, and thus facilitate the displacement of aggression elsewhere; (3) masochistically submit to the patient's assault with an eventual acting out of his aggression; or (4) oscillate between attempting to resolve the patient's hatred analytically and emotionally giving up on the patient.

> These natural oscillations may actually reflect a reasonable compromise formation that permits the therapist to step back and evaluate the effects of his various interventions and gives him some breathing space before he returns to an active interpretive stance. [Kernberg 1992, p. 31]

Approaching specific technical interventions, Kernberg makes the following seven suggestions: (1) assess the realistic risks of unleashing destructive forces from within the patient and the possibility of their being contained by the patient's ego and the therapeutic frame; (2) judiciously use various auxiliary measures, including a firm initial contract (Kernberg et al. 1989, Yeomans et al. 1992), to structure the treatment in order to minimize risks to the patient, therapist, and others; (3)

diagnose secondary defenses against hatred and consistently interpret them, with full awareness that such interventions might shift a quiet psychopathic transference (involving deceptiveness, dishonesty, and deliberate withholding of information) to a more heated paranoid one; (4) help the patient become aware of his pleasure in hatred, thus seeking to render it ego-dystonic; (5) interpret the patient's paranoid reaction including acknowledging the incompatible views of "reality" held by the patient and the therapist; (6) identify, circumscribe, and tolerate such a "psychotic nucleus" in the transference before attempting to resolve it interpretively; and (7) interpret, in a relatively traditional manner, the guilt-ridden depressive transferences that emerge after the resolution of paranoid transferences.

Kernberg's focus is on interpretation, and the ancillary measures suggested by him are intended to sustain this unmasking interpretive enterprise. His approach is steadfastly consistent with his theory and unwaveringly "classic" (Strenger 1989), despite its overtones of much activity on the therapist's part. However, while emphasizing the necessity to discern defenses *against* hatred, Kernberg does not pay adequate attention to the alternate formulation, that is, the defensive functions *of* hatred (e.g., against dependent longings in the transference). And, while in his phenomenological outline he notes the characterological anchoring of hatred, he does not address the adaptive aspect of transference hatred. The issue, I must emphasize, is not whether hatred in transference is an activation of an early victim–victimizer relationship (however distorted by fantasy) or is itself a defense against "the dread to resourceless dependence" (Khan 1972). It is not an either/or situation since "in the flow and flux of analytic material we are always in the world of 'both/and' " (Wallerstein 1983, p. 31). I admire Dr. Kernberg's consistent focus on the first formulation while questioning his omission of the second one.

Similarly, in his emphasis on interpretation, Kernberg seems to minimize the analyst's other functions, such as the role of the "holding environment" (Winnicott 1960). While Kernberg does acknowledge the need of structuring the treatment, his focus is more on the realistic risks and not on the psychic containment and metabolism of the patient's hatred by the analyst (see the elaboration of technical consequences of the holding environment concept in Akhtar 1992a, Lewin and Schulz 1992, Modell 1976). Kernberg also does not discern the unconscious hope inherent in the patient's hatred, a hope that the analyst will survive his attacks and, in doing so, detoxify his relentless need for revenge. Pao (1965) observes that "when a patient allows himself to reveal his affective state, the patient is more committed to attempting a constructive personality change" (p. 263). Also, in recommending consistent interpretation, Kernberg seems to overlook that the patient in throes of intense hatred often does not have a reasonable portion of his ego allied with the analyst. The patient is not receptive to the interpretive undertaking. "When deeply regressed, the patient can not identify with the analyst or appreciate his point of view anymore than the fetus or newly born can sympathize with the mother" (Winnicott 1947, p. 202).

Kernberg also does not address the possibility that the patient's expression of hatred might actually be a developmental milestone, achieved for the first time during the analytic situation. Kramer (1987) has made a similar point about the emergence of a sense of entitlement for the first time during analysis. Under such circumstances, a quick effort at interpretive resolution is perhaps not the most suitable element of technique. More helpful, at first, is a "developmental interpretation" (Abrams 1978) that supports and helps structuralize the resumption of hitherto thwarted initiatives in the patient. Putting all this together, it appears that Kernberg's logical interpretive stance leaves little space for containment, holding, validating, affirming, and development-facilitating sorts of interventions. (To be sure, some other analysts, such as Balint, Winnicott, and Kohut tend to lean too heavily in the opposite direction.) Once again, it is not an "either/or" argument but a "both/and" plea. A synthesis of the two technical stances does seem warranted.

Similar broad-mindedness is needed in conceptualizing the hatred experienced by the analyst. Kernberg traces its origin to the patient's assault and to his use of splitting and projective identification. In other words, the hatred felt by the analyst is actually the patient's hatred. I agree with this formulation but, seeing additional possibilities, find it restrictive. Nina Coltart tersely addresses this very issue.

> The belief that whatever happens in the psychoanalytic process is a result of something emanating from the patient, which is then projected into the analyst, has contributed to the creation of a distinctively stagnant psychoanalytic product: the "you-mean-me" interpretation. . . . "You-mean-me" interpretations automatically refer everything that the patient says to a comment about the analyst. Such comments are then said to be "transference-interpretations." In fact they represent a certain paranoid position on the part of the analyst, systematized and presented under the useful disguise of good, "depressive," "maternal" work. [Coltart, in Kohon 1986, p. 72]

What could be the other sources of the therapist's hatred? First, his own conflicts, independent of those of the patient, might generate hatred in him. Second, marked actual differences in ethical and political spheres between the two parties might actually or defensively be stirred up in the analyst, causing him to experience hatred. Third, since hatred is "not always pathological" (Kernberg 1992, p. 23), the therapist's hatred of his patient might also (either totally or in part) be at times rational. Indeed, Winnicott (1947) not only speaks of the therapist's justified hate but also of the technical implications of such conceptualization. He proposes that

> in certain stages of certain analyses the analyst's hate is actually
> sought by the patient, and what is then needed is hate that is
> objective. If the patient seeks objective or justified hate he must
> be able to reach it, else he can not feel he can reach objective
> love. [p. 199]

Winnicott bases this technical stance upon his sense that a growing child can only believe in being loved after reaching being hated; here, he echoes Freud's (1913) statement that "in the order of development hate is the precursor of love" (p. 325). Winnicott goes on to raise the matter of disclosure of the analyst's hate to the patient:

> This is obviously a matter fraught with danger, and it needs
> the most careful timing. But I believe an analysis is incomplete
> if even towards the end it has not been possible for the analyst
> to tell the patient what he, the analyst, did unbeknown for the
> patient whilst he was ill, in the early stages. Until this inter-
> pretation is made the patient is kept to some extent in the
> position of infant—one who can not understand what he owes
> to his mother. [p. 202]

The omission of the therapist's objective hatred and its ultimate revelation, guided by considerations of optimal distance (Akhtar 1992b, Bouvet 1958, Escoll 1992) and tact (Poland 1975), is noticeable in Kernberg's technical recommendations. Risking the "sin of repetition" (Kiell 1988, p. 2), I emphasize that the technical notions I have tried to highlight here are additive, *not* alternative, to what Dr. Kernberg suggests. The view of patient's hatred as an activation of an early object relationship, the conceptualization of the therapist's hatred as a countertransference response, and the consistent focus on interpretation are enriched, not impoverished, by comparable attention to the defensive and adaptive aspects of the patient's hatred, the objective nature of the analysts' hatred, and the role of noninterpretive interventions during the treatment. In attempting a synthesis of this sort, the risk of wishy-washiness must be boldly faced if the ultimate reward of informed eclecticism is to be deserved.

CONCLUDING REMARKS

In conclusion, I come back to the richness, breadth, and profound clinical value of Kernberg's chapter. In the realm of hatred, he has offered us penetrating insights regarding the complex ties between the genetically preprogrammed neurochemical apparatuses and pathways on the one hand, and childhood trauma, its fantasy elaboration, consolidation through affects, and repetitions in life and treatment situations on the other hand. Kernberg's propositions are powerful and convincing. Yet some areas remain unclear. Among them, the following four especially stand out.

First, there seems a discrepancy in Kernberg's schemes of the evolution and organization of sexual and aggressive drives. In the sexual realm he (1991) suggests a three-step process consisting of "sexual excitement," "erotic desire," and "love." In the aggressive realm, however, he proposes a two-step process only, progressing from "rage" to "hatred." Sexual excitement is the core affect of libido, rage the core affect of aggression. Erotic desire is the higher-level affect state of libido, hatred the higher-level affect state of aggression. This leaves us with no counterpart of love in the aggressive realm. Since an aesthetics of symmetry usually accompanies Kernberg's theorizing, this discrepancy draws attention.

Second, while Kernberg emphasizes the sustained nature of hatred, Anna Freud (1972) has a different stance. She feels that while libidinal aims are specific to the drive, aggressive aims associate themselves with varying purposes. She also distinguishes the two drives in regard to the objects. Libidinal development proceeds from a need-satisfying object through intermediate steps to object constancy, but aggression does not take this step toward sustained commitment. The seemingly "fixed hate" (A. Freud 1962, p. 165) of the paranoic is actually a vicissitude of libido rather than of aggression.[3] According to Anna Freud, a good lover is faithful, a good hater promiscuous.[4] How is this observation to be integrated with Kernberg's view of hatred as closely tied to a specific object representation?

Third, the antagonistic relationship between hatred and forgiveness needs to be fleshed out. Are there intermediary stages between the two extremes? Are there traumas that are unforgivable and yet do not fuel sustained hatred? With what affects are they associated? What is the impact of hatred on memory and how do alterations in memory of past "reality" facilitate a move towards acceptance and forgiveness? Kafka's (1989) view that we repeat not what we have repressed and cannot remember but what we remember in a particular rigid way is pertinent here. See also Volkan's (1987, 1988) psychopolitical observations in this regard. Rudolph and Rudolph (1993) have, in contrast, argued that memories of old hurts are often dredged up to create "ancient hatreds" out of contemporary socioeconomic conflicts.

---

3. Blum's (1981) concept of the "inconstant object" is a contemporary elaboration of this "fixed hate" theme. It refers to an ambivalently loved object that is felt as both persecutory and needed. It cannot be allowed to have a separate existence. The threat of betrayal by it must be tenaciously maintained. In a sense, such constant fear of persecution is the reciprocal of libidinal object constancy and a desperate effort to preserve an illusory constant object.

4. A social observation supporting the promiscuous nature of hate is that individuals with pronounced anti-Semitism also despise other ethnic minorities (Adorno and Frenkel-Brunswick 1950). Significantly, a replication of this American study in India (Varma et al. 1973) revealed similar results regarding the distribution of anti-Muslim attitudes.

Fourth, Kernberg states that hatred is not always pathological and, in those with normal superego integration, it
"bridges over to the sublimatory function of courageous
aggressive assertion in the service of commitment to ideals
and ethical systems" (Kernberg 1992, p. 25). Others (e.g.,
Horowitz, in Winer 1994, Winnicott 1947) agree with the
concept of "normal hatred." Indeed, Thomas Carlyle
(1795–1881) cheerily quipped about "a healthy hatred of
scoundrels," and Freud's lifelong "need for an enemy" (Gay
1988, p. 396) underscored the existential value of such hatred.
Long before both of them, Aristotle, in *Nicomachean Ethics*,
had already voiced a similar sentiment: "To enjoy the things
we ought and to hate the things we ought has the greatest
bearing on excellent character." However, more clarity is
needed here. What really are the characteristics of the so-
called normal hatred? Is the incapacity to feel it pathological?
Are there cross-cultural variations of it? Are there developmental phases (e.g., adolescence) when hatred is more "normal" than at other times (e.g., latency)? Winnicott (1947) does
talk about the structure-building role of objective hatred
between parents and children, but we need to know more
about this "good enough hate" (Harvey Rich, personal communication).

I conclude with a brief quotation from an unlikely source,
which captures the complexity of the phenomena under consideration. It hints at the traumatic origins of hatred, the
powerful rationalizations and their accompanying ego and
superego distortions, the mechanisms of splitting, denial, and
projective identification, the affective and cognitive hell of
paranoia, and the ultimately self-destructive results of hatred.
This was spoken by the late Richard Nixon on August 9,
1974, the day he resigned in disgrace from the Presidency of
the United States of America: "Others may hate you. Those
who hate you don't win unless you hate them. And then you
destroy yourself!"

REFERENCES

Abrams, S. (1978). The teaching and learning of psychoanalytic developmental psychology. *Journal of the American Psychoanalytic Association* 26:387–406.

Adorno, J., and Frenkel-Brunswick, E. (1950). *The Authoritarian Personality*. New York: W. W. Norton.

Akhtar, S. (1990). Paranoid personality disorder. *American Journal of Psychotherapy* 44:5–25.

_____ (1991). Three fantasies related to unresolved separation-individuation: a less recognized aspect of severe character pathology. In *Beyond The Symbiotic Orbit: Advances in Separation-Individuation Theory—Essays in Honor of Selma Kramer, M.D.*, ed. S. Akhtar and H. Parens, pp. 261–284. Hillsdale, NJ: The Analytic Press.

_____ (1992a). *Broken Structures: Severe Personality Disorders and Their Treatment*. Northvale, NJ: Jason Aronson.

_____ (1992b). Tethers, orbits and invisible fences: clinical, developmental, sociocultural, and technical aspects of optimal distance. In *When the Body Speaks: Psychological Meanings in Kinetic Clues*, ed. S. Kramer and S. Akhtar, pp. 21–57. Northvale, NJ: Jason Aronson.

_____ (1994). Object constancy and adult psychopathology. *International Journal of Psycho-Analysis* 75:441–455.

_____ (in press). Aggression: theories regarding its nature and origins. In *Psychoanalysis: The Major Concepts*, ed. B. Moore and B. Fine. New Haven: Yale University Press.

Berliner, B. (1958). The role of object relations in moral masochism. *Psychoanalytic Quarterly* 27:38–56.

Blum, H. P. (1981). Object inconstancy and paranoid conspiracy. *Journal of the American Psychoanalytic Association* 29:789–813.

Bouvet, M. (1958). Technical variation and the concept of distance. *International Journal of Psycho-Analysis* 39:211–221.

Deutsch, H. (1942). Some forms of emotional disturbance and their relationship to schizophrenia. *Psychoanalytic Quarterly* 11:301–321.

Escoll, P. J. (1992). Vicissitudes of optimal distance through the life cycle. In *When the Body Speaks: Psychological Meanings in Kinetic Clues*, ed. S. Kramer and S. Akhtar, pp. 59–87. Northvale, NJ: Jason Aronson.

Fairbairn, W. R. D. (1940). Schizoid factors in the personality. In *An Object Relations Theory of Personality*, pp. 3–27. New York: Basic Books, 1952.

Fenichel, O. (1954). The ego and the affects. In *The Collected Papers*, 2nd series, pp. 215–227. New York: W. W. Norton.

Freud, A. (1972). Comments on aggression. *International Journal of Psycho-Analysis* 53:163–171.

Freud, S. (1913). The disposition to obsessional neurosis. *Standard Edition* 12:311–326.

_____ (1920). Beyond the pleasure principle. *Standard Edition* 18:7–64.

Galdston, R. (1987). The longest pleasure: a psychoanalytic study of hatred. *International Journal of Psycho-Analysis* 68:371.

Gay, P. (1988). *Freud: A Life for Our Time*. New York: W. W. Norton.

Hill, L. B. (1938). The use of hostility as a defense. *Psychoanalytic Quarterly* 7:254–264.

Jacobson, E. (1953). The affects and their pleasure–unpleasure qualities in relation to the psychic discharge processes. In *Drives, Affects, Behavior*, ed. R. M. Loewenstein. New York: International Universities Press.

Jones, E. (1929). Fear, guilt, and hate. In *Papers on Psychoanalysis*. Baltimore, MD: Williams and Wilkins, 1950.

Kafka, J. (1989). *Multiple Realities in Clinical Practice*. New Haven: Yale University Press.

Kernberg, O. F. (1975). *Borderline Conditions and Pathological Narcissism*. New York: Jason Aronson.

——— (1984). *Severe Personality Disorders: Psychotherapeutic Strategies*. New Haven: Yale University Press.

——— (1989). The narcissistic personality disorder and the differential diagnosis of antisocial behavior. *The Psychiatric Clinics of North America* 12:553–570.

——— (1991). Sadomasochism, sexual excitement and perversion. *Journal of the American Psychoanalytic Association* 39:333–362.

——— (1992). *Aggression in Personality Disorders and Perversions*. New Haven: Yale University Press.

Kernberg, O. F., Selzer, M. A., Koenigsberg, H. W., et al. (1989). *Psychodynamic Psychotherapy of Borderline Patients*. New York: Basic Books.

Khan, M. (1972). Dread of surrender to resourceless dependence in the analytic situation. In *The Privacy of the Self*. New York: International Universities Press, 1974.

Kiell, N. (1988). *Freud Without Hindsight: Reviews of His Work 1893–1939*. New York: International Universities Press.

Kohon, G. (1986). *The British School of Psychoanalysis: The Independent Tradition*. New Haven: Yale University Press.

Kramer, S. (1987). A contribution to the concept "the exception" as a developmental phenomenon. *Journal of Abuse and Neglect* 11:367–370.

Kundera, M. (1990). *Immortality*. New York: Grove Weidenfeld.

Lewin, R. A., and Schulz, C. (1992). *Losing and Fusing: Borderline Transitional Object and Self Relations*. Northvale, NJ: Jason Aronson.

Lichtenberg, J. D. (1989). *Psychoanalysis and Motivation*. Hillsdale, NJ: Analytic Press.

Mahler, M. S., Pine, F., Bergman, A. (1975). *The Psychological Birth of the Human Infant*. New York: Basic Books.

Maltsberger, J. T., and Buie, D. H. (1974). Countertransference hate in the treatment of suicidal patients. *Archives of General Psychiatry* 30:625–633.

Modell, A. (1976). The holding environment and the therapeutic action of psychoanalysis. *Journal of the American Psychoanalytic Association* 24:285–307.

Pao, P. N. (1965). The role of hatred in the ego. *Psychoanalytic Quarterly* 34:257–264.

Poland, W. S. (1975). Tact as a psychoanalytic function. *International Journal of Psycho-Analysis* 56:155.

Rudolph, S. H., and Rudolph, L. I. (1993). Modern hate. *The New Republic*, March 22, pp. 24–29.

Searles, H. F. (1956). The psychodynamics of vengefulness. *Psychiatry* 19:31–39.

——— (1962). Scorn, disillusionment and adoration in the psychotherapy of schizophrenia. *Psychoanalytic Review* 49:39–60.

Shapiro, D. (1965). *Neurotic Styles*. New York: Basic Books.

Strenger, C. (1989). The classic and romantic visions in psychoanalysis. *International Journal of Psycho-Analysis* 70:595–610.

Varma, V. K., Akhtar, S., and Kulhara, P. N. (1973). Measurement of authoritarian traits in India. *Indian Journal of Psychiatry* 15:156–175.

Volkan, V. D. (1987). Psychological concepts in political foundations between nations. *Journal of the American Psychoanalytic Association* 35:903.

_____ (1988). *The Need to Have Enemies and Allies*. Northvale, NJ: Jason Aronson.

Wallerstein, R. S. (1983). Self psychology and "classical" psychoanalytic psychology: the nature of their relationship. In *The Future of Psychoanalysis*, ed. A. Goldberg, pp. 19–63. New York: International Universities Press.

Winer, J. A. (1994). Panel report: hate in the analytic setting. *Journal of the American Psychoanalytic Association* 42:219–232.

Winnicott, D. W. (1947). Hate and the countertransference. In *Collected Papers: Through Pediatrics to Psychoanalysis*, pp. 194–203. London: Tavistock, 1958.

_____ (1960). Ego distortion in terms of true and false self. In *The Maturational Processes and the Facilitating Environment*, pp. 73–82. New York: International Universities Press.

Yeomans, F. E., Selzer, M. A., and Clarkin, J. F. (1992). *Treating the Borderline Patient: A Contract-Based Approach*. New York: Basic Books.

6

ON THE ORIGIN AND EVOLUTION OF A SPECIES OF HATE: A CLINICAL-LITERARY EXCURSION

Fred Pine, PH.D.

An explanation of the title will provide an introduction to the content and method of this chapter, in which I describe a species of hate that I have encountered a number of times in my clinical work and in my supervision of the work of others. I have no reason to believe that there are not other species, but this is one that I have come to see frequently—perhaps by chance, or perhaps because it is indeed a more frequent form. My experience with it is in females. The core phenomenon— the "origin of the species" one might say—is a young daughter's encounter with her mother's repeated rages. The rage takes such a form that the child feels depersonalized, foreign to the mother, reduced, like an object.[1] The child's experience is that the mother has become a different person, forgetting that the child is her child. The rage is experienced as being directed against the child in her very personhood, not at something

---

1. In this chapter, I generally use the term *object* in its nonpsychoanalytic sense: a thing, without inner experience that matters.

specific that she has done that can be changed (though that may be the trigger), but against her very being. And she feels helpless to do anything about it. These two features—being reduced and objectified and the helplessness to affect it—are the defining ones.

The impact of such experiences in childhood in at least some instances produces hate, but the hate evolves over time, as we shall see. Hate takes variant forms in adult women who have had that childhood history, and the adult phenomenon is a residue of that history.

In the interest of preserving confidentiality, I am not citing clinical material from my own practice or from that of those I have supervised. But literature—novels and plays— can provide suitable case material. I have asked friends who were writers or professors of English literature to suggest works to me in which women who hate were described. I told them (based on my clinical experience) some of the various forms that that hate may take. Their suggestions have pro- vided the case material for this chapter. Thus, my subtitle, "A Clinical-Literary Excursion."

When the literature cited does not match my own clinical experience, I shall point that out. Interestingly, the main place where that happens is in the stories of women who hate because of being dominated by a world of men. While I have not seen this as a *primary* source of hate in female patients, it is of interest that the features of being treated like an object and reduced in one's personhood, as well as a perceived or real helplessness to affect this, characterize the position of these women in male-dominated society, just as those features characterize the position of the female patients as children. Perhaps the fit is not accidental; perhaps the conditions of reduced humanness and helplessness to affect it are central onset conditions for the development of hate—in the family, in society, in the concentration camp, and under sadistic and threatening regimes everywhere. Hate need not be the only response to this, but this may nonetheless be one prototypic origin of hate. And the fact that I have seen this more in females, in my clinical experience, may point to some code-termination by familial and societal experiences in at least some instances.

I do not doubt that overlapping and contradictory ideas can be found in the professional psychoanalytic literature. I will leave that to the reader to discover.

Let's start by citing the dictionary definition of *hate* (*Webster's Ninth New College Dictionary*, 1984):

> *Hate*: Intense hostility and aversion, usually deriving from fear, anger, or sense of injury. Synonyms: detest, abhor, abominate, loathe. [All] mean to feel strong aversion or intense dislike for. Hate implies an emotional aversion often coupled with enmity or malice; detest suggests violent antipathy; abhor implies a deep, often shuddering, repugnance; abominate suggests strong detestation and often moral condemnation; loathe implies utter disgust and intolerance.

The relation of hate to anger is something like that of moods to specific affects—that is, extended in time and space. Hate is a long-lasting and widespread seething state, occasionally breaking through to the surface in rage, sadism, or subtler forms of hatefulness.

A LITERARY EXCURSION

Euripides: *Medea*

Medea, along with her two sons, has been abandoned by Jason, her husband, their father, who marries the daughter of Creon, King of Corinth. In revenge, Medea kills her two sons and also causes the deaths of the princess and her father, the king.

We first learn of Medea in a soliloquy by the children's nurse and a conversation between the nurse and the children's tutor. She is introduced ominously. "I am afraid some dreadful purpose is forming in her mind" (p. 18)[2] after Jason's betrayal. "Don't let [the boys] go to her. I've watched her watching them, her eye like a wild bull's . . . and I know this: she'll not relax her rage until it has found its victim" (p. 20).

The nurse has her theory regarding the source of Medea's state. "Sorrow," she says, "is the real cause of deaths and disasters and families destroyed" (p. 23). By suggesting sorrow, she seems to be implying that loss (of Jason)—or loss plus some unspecified pain—has moved Medea.

Jason has a different theory: sexual jealousy. First, he self-justifyingly explains that he meant well by his two sons— remarrying wealth and power so that they would be the gainers. And then he goes on to accuse Medea, and all women, of feeling content if their sexual life is satisfactory, but becoming jealous and destructive when that is not the case.

But Medea's internal experience is different from either of these. It is, instead, an experience of being slighted, insulted, mocked, reduced. Here, after all of the killings, in brief (before I quote more extensively) is the final exchange between Medea and Jason, in which they talk past one another, Jason only hearing his view of Medea's actions as a response to his leaving her to sleep with another, Medea emphasizing the insult to her sense of self. Jason: "It was not my hand that killed my sons." Medea: "No, not your hand; but your insult to me, and your new-wedded wife." Jason: "You thought that reason enough to murder them, that I no longer slept with you?" And in a final ambiguity, Medea answers: "And is that injury a slight one, do you imagine, to a woman?" (p. 59). I say "ambiguity" because it could sound as though she is agreeing

---

2. All page numbers for quotations are from the edition of the literary work listed in the references.

with Jason that the source is sexual jealousy ("is that injury a slight one?"), but she has, I believe, refocused the issue onto her inner state, that of being *injured*. The play has led up to this view of things.

Medea's internal experience is a compound of a sense of injury—a sense that builds to imagined public humiliation—and a sense of righteousness. It is powerfully expressed in a number of passages. At her first appearance onstage: "Am I not wronged? . . . Children, your mother is hated" (p. 20). Soon thereafter: "Do you see how I am used . . . by my accursed husband? Oh, may I see Jason and his bride ground to pieces in their shattered palace for the wrong they have dared to do to me" (p. 22).

The righteousness implied here in "the wrong they have *dared* to do to me" has struck me clinically. It is a frequent accompaniment of hate and hate-based rage. I think it stems from something self-preservative ("I have been so mistreated that I have this right . . .") and some flaw in the superego, possibly based on identification with the child's experience of the rageful mother's giving herself full permission—and without subsequent remorse—to express her rage toward the child. Of course, in *Medea*, as in much of the literature I shall describe, we do not know the early mother–child history.

Medea says to Jason, "How we are besmirched and mocked by this man's broken vows, and all our hopes deceived" (p. 32). And, after explaining that she will kill her children to wound Jason and Jason's new wife and her father, King Creon: "Yes, I can endure guilt, however horrible; the laughter of my enemies I will not endure" (p. 41). Whence this sense of being mocked, laughed at? In the clinical situation I have wondered if the child senses some pleasure component, that is, some sadism, some scorn, in the mother's attack.

After saying she will cause the second wife to "die a hideous death," Medea says, "Let no one think of me as humble or weak or passive. I am of a different kind: dangerous to my enemies; loyal to my friends. To such a life glory belongs" (p. 42). But what is this "glory"? It is all imaginary. The glory she speaks of is *not* in the eyes of others, but is her internal experience of power, of survival, of reversal following the experience of humiliation.

What we sense in Medea is a long-simmering sense of injustice, of propensity toward humiliation, and with these a propensity toward rage. In her, it is accompanied by righteousness and exhilaration. These are the elements of her hatred of Jason.

The relations between the sexes serve the explanatory purpose that the parent–child relationship serves clinically. We see that, too, in Medea. After bemoaning the fact that Jason's betrayal has destroyed her life and happiness, she goes on to say:

> "Surely, of all creatures that have life and will, we women are the most wretched. When, for an extravagant sum, we have bought a husband, we must then accept him as possessor of our body. This is to aggravate wrong with worse wrong" (p. 24). And "Besides—we were born woman—useless for honest purposes, but in all kinds of evil skilled practitioners" (p. 29).

I do not mean to suggest that hate cannot grow from these relations between the sexes—possession of the body experienced as reduction of personhood—but that in my particular clinical experience the emphasis has been instead overwhelmingly on early parent–child versions of these same issues.

Euripides: *Elektra*

The hate in Elektra is more complex, having none of the single-mindedness, the righteousness (how "dare" they), the irrationality (the killing of innocent children), nor the self-referential antecedents ("the laughter of my enemies I will not endure") of Medea's hate. Nor do other characters in the play see Elektra primarily as hating, but rather as wronged. Here, interestingly, "wronged" has reference not to an internal subjective state but to an actuality, an event in the real world—the murder of her father.

Clytemnestra, mother of Orestes and Elektra, has killed their father, Agamemnon, upon his return from the Trojan Wars, in order to marry Aegisthus and share the throne with him. Both Orestes and Elektra, in different ways, instill fear of revenge in Aegisthus, and both have been banished from their home. The action of the play takes place when Orestes returns secretly to his homeland, finds Elektra, and the two plot the murders of Aegisthus and Clytemnestra—Aegisthus's murder by Orestes and (although Elektra had said "the killing of my mother I shall claim for myself" [p. 127]) Clytemnestra's apparently by them both.

Whereas Medea is a hating (and hateful) figure—with a history of other killings and betrayals even prior to the action of the Jason-Medea tragedy—Elektra is a sympathetic figure throughout. If there be hate here, it is clearly of a different quality. In order not to bear royal sons who might avenge themselves on Aegisthus and displace him, Elektra has been forced to marry a peasant (in a marriage that was never consummated). She holds the memory of her mother's deed and, when the time comes, she is the one to insist that Clytemnestra be killed (in the face of Orestes' doubts).

Yet, she is given by Euripides two long, carefully reasoned speeches (not ranting, not personalized), in one of which she in effect outlines the historical case against Aegisthus (p. 136 ff) and in the other (to her face) against Clytemnestra (p. 141 ff). Elektra also gives reasoned rebuttal to Clytemnestra's claim that she killed Agamemnon because he sacrificed their daughter, Iphigenia, at Aulis (p. 140).

So, again, *hate* is a term that we may choose to use or not

use here. Elektra carries a wish and an obligation to avenge her
father's death, and she carries a sense of having been cruelly
wronged. Though married off to a peasant (and thus
wronged), she does not feel reduced in her humanity—objectified—but rather seems to understand her banishment more
as a political act motivated by Aegisthus' fear (though it is
clear she holds her mother particularly responsible) and in fact
sees her peasant husband as more respectful and noble than the
noblemen involved in the tragedy.

As the time for the murders approaches and they are
carried out and especially in relation to the murder of the
mother, the emotional situation becomes more complex. Not
righteousness, but ambivalence, doubt, remorse, guilt enter
in. That is, the victim is not "reduced"—one feels for the
victim—because the murderer has not felt reduced. This holds
even in reverse, for Clytemnestra herself. Speaking to Elektra
(after Elektra's condemnation of her) she says: "My child,
your nature has always been to love your father. It is natural;
some children love their fathers best, and some their mothers.
I'll forgive you. I do not in fact exult unduly over what I did.
With what insensate fury I drove myself to take my grand
revenge! How bitterly I regret it now!" (p. 142).

Elektra's inner situation immediately after the murder of
Clytemnestra is also complex—not righteous, not victorious,
none of the "glory" felt by Medea. Thus, immediately after
Orestes speaks of his tears for his deed, Elektra speaks: "Tears,
my brother—let tears be endless. I am guilty. I was burning
with desperate rage against her; yet she was my mother, I her
daughter" (pp. 145–146). The chorus, until now understanding the need for justice to be done, now blames Elektra
(but softly, and modified by "dear"): "Dear Elektra, you did a
dreadful wrong to your brother, forcing him against his will
[to kill Clytemnestra]" (p. 146). And just prior to that, after
Elektra begins to see the consequences of her act, the chorus
speaks: "Your mind has returned to itself and blows now with

the wind of truth" (p. 146). And Elektra soon speaks again, as she covers her mother's body: "As we wrap this cloak around you we love you, though we hated you" (pp. 147–148).

In a closing scene, Castor, son of Zeus, speaks for the Gods—again a complex rendering: "Her fate [Clytemnestra's] was just; but your act is not justified" (p. 148). There is recognition of sorrow, of regret, and not only of guilt and criminality. And both Orestes and Elektra are instructed how to pay for, and thus expiate, their crime (or sin).

So, one may think of Elektra's long-standing wish to avenge her father's death, and her ability to carry through the deed of murdering her mother, as reflective of hate. But it is a hatred different from Medea's. The species of hate we are discussing is one built around feeling reduced and objectified, and helpless to affect it; but this is not true of Elektra. There are, no doubt, other species of hate; perhaps Elektra's is one of those.

Eugene O'Neill: *Mourning Becomes Electra*

In psychoanalytic theory, the term *Elektra complex* has sometimes been used as the parallel form, for the female, of the *Oedipus complex*. And one may, with the Elektra of Euripides, say that the appeal of the play is because of its match with unconscious matricidal fantasies stemming from childhood, as Freud said regarding the Oedipus complex. But Euripides, in my reading, does not give place to rivalrous motivations from the childhood period in his telling of the story. O'Neill, writing after Freud, certainly does do this in his retelling of the legend. And the hate here is of the kind I am addressing.

Mourning Becomes Electra is a play in the form of a trilogy (*The Homecoming*, *The Hunted*, *The Haunted*) in which the oedipal theme is paramount. Lavinia (Electra) loves her father, Brigadier General Ezra Mannon (Agamemnon), and hates her mother, Christine (Clytemnestra), with a jealous passion.

This triangle is replayed in the love of both women for Adam Brant, Christine's lover. And it is further replayed in the deep attachment of Christine and her son, Orin (Orestes), who in turn hates his father, whom he feels to be uncaring. The tragedy moves swiftly through the killing of Ezra by Christine (to rid herself of him and to free her for Brant), the discovery by Lavinia (Electra) of both the killing of her father and her mother's affair with Brant, the revenge killing of Brant by Lavinia and Orin, and Lavinia's and Orin's (each in their own way) driving Christine to suicide.

O'Neill, in contrast to Euripides, makes the apparently oedipal theme explicit—Lavinia's love for her father (and Brant) and her jealous hatred of her mother in relation to both. Even at the moment of killing Brant—supposedly in retaliation for his role in Christine's murder of Ezra, her father— Lavinia (with a switch from the overt to the covert motivation) says to Brant: "How could you love that vile old woman so?" (p. 802). The final section, after the murder of Ezra and the suicide of Christine—called *The Haunted*—moves compellingly from the fear of the ignorant townspeople that the Mannon house is haunted by ghosts, to the emergence of the "ghosts" that haunt Lavinia and Orin, as they find themselves repeating the behaviors of their parents. The result is uncanny in its effect upon the reader.

The hate in the play is described primarily in the first part of the trilogy, as the relationship between Lavinia and Christine unfolds. It is clearly based on a lifetime of jealous rivalry in Lavinia, and with Christine feeling from the start that Lavinia was Ezra's child, not her own—so hateful did she find the sexual contact with Ezra (again the hatred based on the sexual possession of the woman by the man). In one scene, Lavinia is speaking to Christine, after having discovered Christine's adultery with Adam Brant and realizing that Christine (as a ruse) had been implying that Brant was really visiting their home because of his interest in Lavinia.

> *Lavinia* (furiously) [O'Neill's stage notes]: How can you lie like that? How can you be so vile as to try to use me to hide your adultery? . . . Stop lying I tell you! . . . I heard you telling him, "I love you Adam" . . . and kissing him! (with a cold bitter fury) You vile—! You're shameless and evil! Even if you are my mother I say it!" (Christine stares at her, overwhelmed by this onslaught, her poise shattered for the moment . . .) (p. 713).

The scene develops with Christine acknowledging her love for Adam and Lavinia again attacking her, now for her shamelessness. Christine seeks to explain herself, telling Lavinia (in a fury) that she has always hated her husband, a hate compounded by her having to submit to him sexually. Lavinia is repulsed and cannot listen. But it finally dawns on her, and she stammers: "You—then you've always hated Father?" (p. 714).

And the scene continues:

> *Christine* (bitterly): No. I loved him once—before I married him—incredible as that seems now! . . . But marriage soon turned . . . romance into disgust!"
> *Lavinia* (wincing again—stammers harshly): So I was born of your disgust. I've always guessed that, Mother—ever since I was little—when I used to come to you—with love— but you would always push me away! I've felt it ever since I can remember—your disgust! (Then with a flare-up of bitter hatred) Oh, I hate you! It's only right I should hate you!
> *Christine* (shaken, defensively): I tried to love you. I told myself it wasn't human not to love my own child, born of my body. But I never could make myself feel you were born of any body but his! You were always my wedding night to me— and my honeymoon! [p. 714]

The scene then goes on to Christine's love for Orin (Lavinia's brother) and Lavinia's jealousy of that.

Lavinia: So triangular rivalry (mother–father–Lavinia; mother–son–Lavinia; mother–lover–Lavinia) is officially given center stage. But is it that that accounts for the bitter hatred felt by Lavinia? I think not. And already in the scene just quoted we have moved from the self-consciously oedipal cast of the play's motivation to the early disruption of the mother–daughter relationship. While it is not the mother's hate and rage directly at the daughter that reduces Lavinia, makes her feel beyond the reach of her mother's love and helpless to affect it, like some negative object/thing in the mother's eyes, the mother's hate and rage toward the father does permeate her relation to her daughter. I believe we are dealing here with the species of hate—reducing and objectifying the person who is helpless to affect it—that is my focus. Though it is played out in relation to Lavinia's idealization of her father and her jealousy of mother, the early wound, the sensing of the maternal aversion and disgust (and therefore hatred) is made clear. Thus it is not the case that Lavinia is primarily in rivalry with the mother for the *father's* love, but is in rivalry with Orin and Brant for her *mother's* love.

Late in the first part of the trilogy the seesawing between these two levels of motivation is made clear. Brigadier General Mannon has just returned from the war. In a moment of falsity, Christine submits to his kiss. At that moment, Lavinia opens the door, observes them, and says to herself (in an anguish of jealous hatred): "I hate you! You steal even Father's love from me again!" (Then, almost with a sob, hiding her face in her hands) "*Oh, Mother! Why have you done this to me! What harm had I done you?*" (Then—with passionate disgust) "Father, how can you love that shameless harlot?" (Then frenziedly) "I can't bear it! I won't! It's my duty to tell him about her! [That is, about the affair with Brant] I will!" (p. 741, emphasis added).

The first failed relationship with the mother of infancy, hopelessly beyond the child's reach, underlies the subsequent hate.

Honoré de Balzac: *Cousin Bette*

The mother's rage that reduces the child to an object, or her failed love, or violations of the body that again make the person an object—and the sense of helplessness to affect it—seem able to serve as the soil in which hatred, seething and long-lasting, can grow. For Cousin Bette (Lisbeth Fischer) the source lies in her experience of grossly unfair treatment, being raised as second best.

Cousin Bette's hate is compounded of jealousy and the wish for vengeance. The younger, homelier cousin of Adeline Fischer—a beauty as a child and as a woman—Bette is sacrificed (in her upbringing) for her beautiful cousin: Bette working in the fields; Adeline treated as a pet. In childhood, her jealousy was expressed by her scratching at Adeline's beautiful nose and, later, tearing her dresses and crumpling her collars. All of this is only compounded when Adeline makes a wealthy marriage, and Bette is brought to live in Paris with her, at first to find a husband but eventually to work at a trade.

She is described (27 years after this move) as avoiding all public social life so as not to feel a sense of inferiority and shame. She has let herself become a non-person, at least publicly. Instead she ingratiated herself to everyone in the family and was a confidante of all but Adeline, but

> this woman, more closely observed, would have recalled the
> fiercely ungovernable side of the peasant character. She was
> still the child who tried to tear her cousin's nose off and who,
> if she had not learned rational behavior, would perhaps have
> killed her in a paroxysm of jealousy. [p. 45]

A crucial turn in the plot comes with an adult repetition of the childhood situation. Bette is working and lives close to poverty. Adeline has married the Baron Hulot, and they have two children. The daughter, Hortense, is beautiful like her mother. Bette has aided a poor and unsuccessful sculptor. They live in the same rooming house. She is much older than he, feels toward him like a lover, but her age, morality, and virginity keep her instead in a more mother-like relationship to him. But she is possessive and wants him for herself. In a romanticized way, she describes him to Adeline's daughter, Hortense, who falls in love with him at first hearing and later at first sight. Adeline and Hortense together contrive (successfully) to achieve a marriage—without any regard to Bette's feelings. So, as the mother, Adeline, bested the child Bette, Hortense bests the adult Bette. Bette is enraged, her long-simmering hatred of Adeline now burning hotly.

Bette makes an alliance with the courtesan, Valerie Marneffe. She says to her:

> You don't know how they've intrigued against me! . . . You don't know how, since I've been old enough to be conscious of it, I have been sacrificed to Adeline! They slapped me and caressed her. I went dressed like a drudge, she like a lady. I dug the garden, peeled the vegetables, and she never lifted a finger except to arrange her ribbons! . . . For 26 years I have had their leavings . . . And now . . . Adeline is robbing me of my happiness! Adeline! Adeline! I will see you in the dust, fallen lower than I am! Hortense, whom I loved, has betrayed me. [p. 112]

The alliance between Valerie and Bette is the driving force of the remainder of the novel. Valerie will seduce the Baron and, later, the sculptor—thus taking the husbands of both Adeline and Hortense. She also drives the Baron into debt, and then into theft—thus impoverishing the family and bringing it to shame. Bette makes this all possible by continuing as the trusted family confidante—gathering necessary information for Valerie and inciting the corrupt actions of the men. Valerie's motive was financial gain—she had four lovers who provided for her—and Bette's motive was vengeance.

"She was hate and vengeance uncompromising" (p. 117). Her ultimate aim was to reduce the Hulot family to shame and poverty, to marry the Baron's wealthy elder brother, and thus to turn the tables completely—making the Hulot family dependent upon her largesse and forcing *them* to work for a living as she had had to. (Only the death of the elder brother and several rather magical turns in the plot frustrate this aim.)

Bette's feelings about her plot with Valerie were ones of delight, replacing with even greater pleasure her love for the sculptor. "The delights of gratified hatred are among the fiercest and most ardent that the heart can feel. Love is the gold, but hate is the iron, of that mine of emotions that lies within us" (p. 170). And continuing, Balzac makes clear Bette's vicarious pleasures as well (for she had made Valerie the lover of both Adeline's and Hortense's husbands, and she had the relation with Valerie herself, thus a vicarious participation in Valerie's beauty and in her conquests).

Balzac writes:

[Valerie] was the axe, Lisbeth the hand that wielded it; and the hand was striking blow upon rapid blow to demolish [the hated Hulot family]; for hatred continually grows, just as love every day increases, when we love. Love and hatred are passions that feed on their own fuel; but of the two, hatred is the more enduring. Love is limited by our human limits; its strength derives from life and giving. Hate is like death and avarice, a denial, a negation, although active, above human beings and human concerns. Lisbeth, having entered upon the life that was congenial to her nature, was devoting to it the strength of all her faculties. [p. 171]

And what is the origin of the hate here? What we see is envy (or jealousy perhaps) and a sense of being reduced, made second best. Balzac tells us here that real wounds have been inflicted. The early family was unthinking and cruel in its preference for Adeline; and Hortense and Adeline are callous in stealing away the sculptor from Bette. Whatever triangular rivalry there may be regarding *him*, it is clear that the real injury Bette experiences is in the repetition of callous disregard. And Balzac shows us hate as seething—long-lived, not essentially dischargeable, and accompanied by a vivid sense of having been wronged, which continues to justify the hate and give the sanction of conscience to the most "hateful" of actions. When I have seen this clinically, the conflict elements and the transformations of hate have been even more in evidence.

Mary Gaitskill: *Two Girls, Fat and Thin*

Dorothy, the "fat girl" of the title, was reared in a working-class family with a limited connection to the world outside. Her father constantly felt the world to be attacking him, beating him down, and felt it as alien. Her mother was content to stuff Dorothy full of junk food, watching her get fatter and fatter, all the while tying her to herself (the mother) as her sole relationship, isolated from friends. Dorothy herself was caught up in childlike fantasy—not of the schizoid, somewhat bizarre kind—but more of the infantile, Santa Claus kind. She was not reared to be a separate person, "her own" person; already in childhood she was, then, a nonperson, but seemed to drift in it without awareness of her state.

Then, in adolescence, her father starts venting his hate upon her—verbally, then sexually. In an alternating pattern, by day he calls her variants of a "lazy fat slob," useless, worthless, and by night he comes to her bed and uses her sexually, grabbing, squeezing, forcing, with the hate apparent in his passion of sex and abuse. The mother is, of course, "not knowing" about all of this, though we later learn that she knew.

Having managed to leave home for college, and being

miserable there—ostracized, insulted for her weight—Dorothy finds herself alone in her room with her memories one night. And feelings flood forth. The author writes in the first person:

> I felt locked out of my own fat body, as if I were a disembodied set of impulses and electrical discharges, disconnected rage and fear, something like what real humans feel in abandoned houses and call "ghosts." I remembered my father on top of me, mashing my lungs, making my breath smaller and tighter until it barely existed, opening my body with his fingers, infecting me with his smells, his sounds, grinding his skin on mine until it came off as a powder and filtered into my pores, spewing his deepest poison into my blood and cells and came out in my sweat, my urine and shit, even my voice and words. I felt so saturated by his liquid stench, I didn't even think to wash it off when he left. I let it dry on my stomach or chest or ass, as I lay still with tears in my eyes. I sat in my dorm room and thought of taking a knife and cutting my face. I went into the bathroom and turned on the light and took off my shirt to stare at and hate my body. There were pimples on my chest and I welcomed them, wishing they were boils or scars, anything to more fully degrade this body, loathed even by its own parent. I had the fleeting thought that my roommate could come home at any minute, and I hoped she would so that I could display the truth about how loathsome I was and feel her contempt as well as my own. [p. 196]

We have here again a by now familiar picture, the child treated as an object, "de-personed," feeling hated and helpless to affect it. But here, in the surge of feelings and memories that floods her, we see not only the hatred of the father, but one of its simplest transformations—her hatred of herself, that is, her identification with his hate of her. The hate seethes inside. *Something* has to be done with it, because it continues to destroy the person inside.

Christina Stead: *The Man Who Loved Children*

This book is painful to read; the Pollit family is painful to live
with for the space of some 500 pages. Sam Pollit, "the man
who loved children," the husband and father of the Pollit
family, is an infantile, self-centered man, for whom others do
not exist except to fawn on him. He is someone who manages
to destroy all those around him, all under the banner of love
for mankind, science and rationality, and family openness. His
wife Henny (Henrietta) is destroyed. His daughter by his
previous marriage, Louie (Louisa), may or may not be; we do
not know. She is a peculiar yet imaginative young person,
who breaks away in the end—to what, we do not know. And
his six younger children have their fate yet before them,
although the oldest of these (about age 10) is already showing
suicidal fantasies.

While Sam's hate, mercilessly teasing and intruding upon
Louie and espousing his ideology of killing people to purify
the race in the name of science is clear to the reader, although
it comes out indirectly through characterological self-
centeredness—and people who are affected by it may *feel* it but
not quite know what hit them because of his constant mas-
querade (after all, he is the man who loves children)—it is
Henny's, not Sam's, hate that is my focus.

We are, as I see it, given to believe that Henny's hate is
predominantly a product of her marriage to Sam ("the great-
I-am," as she calls this egocentric man) and, beyond that, the
condition of all women. (As noted, this is a common theme in
the works I've read, such as Ibsen's *Hedda Gabler* and perhaps
Strindberg's *Miss Julie*.) Her family and childhood is presented
briefly, but not unsympathetically. She comes from a wealthy
family, although the wealth is squandered. She did not quite
make it as a society belle in Baltimore, and so married Sam—
the child of a poor family who had become a conservationist,

a government bureaucrat, and eventually an unemployed man whose family lives in abject poverty.

While Henny is able to see Sam as a big baby who never grew up, and while she never quite sees what I see as *his* hating and hatefulness, she nonetheless hates him *and her condition*, seen as the slavery and sexual bondage of women. Her hate is simmering and eruptive by turns. She randomly attacks and insults her children and threatens to kill them although her devotion to them is always clear, and they do not fear her. With Louie (Henny's stepdaughter from Sam's first marriage), the verbal attacks and the implication of prior physical beatings are less tempered by love and devotion. There is a strong bond between them and Louie is very loyal to Henny, but Henny's hate is nonetheless more open.

As an aside, Louie draws on Henny's hate in a way that is enlivening for her—and in this she illustrates not quite a transformation that hate may engender but rather some of the extra functions it may come to serve—here, as a self-defining emotion. Louie does not fully experience her own hate, but can by "borrowing" it from Henny. Thus, when Sam and his family (of origin) are clowning in ways that are always without real contact and at the edge of insult, Louie would rush to Henny's room:

> Whenever her irritations got too deep, she mooched in to see her mother. Here, she had learned, . . . was a brackish well of hate to drink from, and a great passion of gall . . . something that put iron in her soul and made her strong to resist the depraved healthiness and idle jollity of the Pollit clan. [p. 258]

But now I turn to Henny's hate of Sam and of her condition as woman. In one of the relatively rare articulate tellings (rather than actings) of her hate in the novel, she is explaining to her friend her impulse to kill Sam, linking it to

his talk about human rights and democracy. But she is infuri-
ated by what she sees as his total use of women. She sums it
up: "It's fine to be a great democrat when you've got a slave to
rub your boots on . . ." (p. 92).

Later, when Sam announces that he is off to Malaya for
months on a work-related trip, leaving her with the care of the
six children, she rages at him, at Louie, all the Pollits, and
marginally at her own children. But then we see one of hate's
transformations—this time into a masochistic power over the
perceived abuser. In the midst of her rage, Henny notices her
wedding ring, realizes Sam is tied to her, cannot just abandon
her, and the author writes:

> For a moment, after years of scamping, she felt the dread
> power of wifehood; they were locked in each other's grasp till
> the end—the end, a mouthful of sunless muckworms and grass
> roots stifling his blare of trumpets and her blasphemies against
> love. The timid, fame-loving wretch would never dare to
> shake her off, and that was how she had him still. [p. 145]

And here is Henny, berating Sam before his family on his
self-important return from Malaya. She had allowed him sex
just before he left and was again pregnant. In an orgy of hate of
him and hate of self she says:

> Look at me! My back's bent in two with the fruit of my womb;
> aren't you sorry to see what happened to me because of his
> lust? I go about with a body like a football, fit to be kicked
> about by a bohunk halfback, an All-American football, be-
> cause of his lust, the fine pure man that won't look at wom-
> en. . . . [and continuing to speak to his family]: To you he's
> something wonderful; if you knew what he is to me, some-
> thing filthy crawling in the sleeve of my dressing gown;
> something dirty, a splotch of blood, or washing up water on
> my skirts. [p. 269]

And a last example: Speaking of her daughter Evie and her stepdaughter Louie, respectively:

> She regarded such a nice, obedient, pretty girl [Evie] as cursed from birth: "Some man will break her or bend her," she always said . . . bitterly; while about Louie she always said, "I'm sorry for the man she marries." About the girls, she only thought of marriage, and about marriage she thought as an ignorant, dissatisfied, but helpless slave did of slavery. [p. 457]

CLINICAL CORRELATIONS

The phenomena I have seen clinically are captured to a degree in the stories I have retold and in the characters whom I've described here. The essences are alike, although in the patients I am thinking of, the degree of transformation of the raw hate is often greater than is represented in the characters here; and, of course, I have access to more personal history, which makes the origin and evolution of the hate more clear.

To summarize the core phenomena as I see them: A psychoanalysis reveals hate to be a central feature, although often in forms not immediately recognizable as such or available to observation. The history reveals early experiences, in the instances that have struck me most clearly, of maternal rages at their daughters (now adult patients). The quality of the rage is such that the child feels distanced from the mother she knew, as though the mother has forgotten that the child is her child. None of the softening of anger that love would bring, or even that personal connection would bring, is experienced as present at these moments. (We, as analysts, might conjecture that the child *is* only an object for the mother at such times—an object in the psychoanalytic sense—when she is playing out something in herself on the child who has become the representative of an internal object or fantasy). And so, not only does the child feel not recognized by the mother, but also fails to recognize the mother[3]—the known mother has gone (although, unfortunately, since these incidents repeat, the foreign, rageful mother also becomes a "known" mother). It is the repetition of these experiences, plus the child's experience of nonhumanness in the eyes of the mother, of nonrelatedness, of being an object and forgotten in its personness, plus also the helplessness to do anything about it, that appeared in the histories of the patients I am familiar with. Although the patients-as-children did not have this word for it, generally, they felt something like hated by the rageful parent at these times. These were rages by mothers (not fathers) at their daughters (the later patients), although I have no reason to believe this need be a general principle.

My own clinical experience does not reveal such instances of hate growing out of adult heterosexual experiences—directly sexual or in a general dominance–submission relation between the sexes. My expectation would be that true sexual brutality could well produce such hate, but that in other instances it might be relations between the sexes as a second version of some earlier hate-inducing relationship that is at the heart of the phenomenon. Nonetheless, I am struck that, in literature, in the not uncommon theme of women's hate for men in connection with specifically sexual or more generally gender relationships, the hate that I have come across has the same features as I have described in the childhood of patients: the sense of being treated unthinkingly, invasively, and as an object, plus the experience of helplessness to affect this.

Though *simmering* hate may thrive and last, the human psyche does not usually live with extremely high-intensity affect states for long periods without some control mecha-

---

3. In a *New York Times Book Review* series on "The Deadly Sins," Mary Gordon (1993) writes about anger—describing a rage of her own that transforms her (as she felt it) into a huge, attacking bird, "a carrion crow." Her son later said to her, "I was scared because I didn't know who you were."

nisms automatically getting set into motion. Clinically, I have seen repeated eruptions of rage as well as transformations of it—all with the original historical context that I have already described. So, going beyond the "origins" of hate in these instances, let me now speak of its "evolution."

In its least altered form, the patient behaves like the mother, raging now at others. The patient is either aware at the outset, or only slowly becomes aware, of this parallel. Aspects of identification and of mastery, turning passive experience to an active one, are both present. But most striking to me is the sometimes accompanying sense of entitlement. Conscience gives its blessing: "this was done to me; now it's my turn." Or, without any self-consciousness, just feeling an inner sense of rightness, of power, of (I would add) correcting an old injury, accompanies the rage.

While for every individual, these rages—like anything else—take on highly individualized meanings and interlock with aspects of the whole character and personality, a second form of the hate is specifically identified by its having taken on additional functions of what feels at the moments of rage like a life-giving source. Again Mary Gordon (1993) describes this:

> Anger is electric, exhilarating. The angry person knows without a doubt he is alive. And the state of unaliveness . . . so frequent and so frightening, . . . that there's no wonder anger feels like treasure. . . . Deadly anger is fanatic of embellishment. . . . The original cause of anger, like the base metal below the ornament, may long have been obscured by the fantastic encrustation. Even the plain desire to hurt may be lost in the detail of the justification for hurting or the elaboration of the punishment. Anger takes on a life of its own, or it divorces itself from life in the service of death dealing, or life denying, or the compulsion to make someone's life unendurable simply for the sake of doing it, simply because it has become the shape of the angry one's life to punish. [p. 3]

   In each of these two forms of direct and "direct plus" expression of hate through rage, conscience gives its blessing to the expression of the hate. There may be regret later, but not necessarily. Conscience could be said, rightly I believe, to be in some way faulted here. But these rages are also an expression of some ultimate "fairness" of conscience in the patients I have seen—a sense of what is right. But "right" refers to the historical situation—either "it was done to me and so I can do it to others, fair is fair," or right because the original mother is in fact the unconscious object of the rage, and so again, "turnabout is fair play." Overall, in all of the patients I have seen, conscience development seems a neces-sary condition for at least this species of hate. It makes possible the sense of injury and therefore rightness, it underlies the control-of-aggression that produces the simmering of hate—each of which is central to the species.

   In another transformation, I have seen the hate appear as an internal persecutor, that is, the hate is experienced as *one's own*, but the accompanying state is not of righteousness, glory, or power, but the polar opposite—utter wrongness. The hate is owned but dreaded. It feels as though it comes like an internal attack. As I understand it, the rage is now experi-enced in its active form—the "I" is the agent—but the sense of victimization by the rage has undergone no transformation, and remains in its passive form—the "I" is the object. It is not that the rage is directed against the self—it has an external object—but the *fact* of the rage attack feels like something beyond one's own control; one is a victim of the rage state.

   In yet a fourth transformation that I have seen, the person—the original child object of the mother's hate—does not hate but behaves hatefully—thus inducing hate in others. Edith Wharton's *Ethan Frome* is told sparely, and moves with a fated inevitability toward its doomed ending. Ethan Frome is poor, and tied to his barely surviving farm and to a series of ill persons under his roof—first his father, then his mother, and, at the time of the novel, his wife Zeena, a self-made chronic invalid. Her cousin, Mattie Silver, has been taken in to care for her—and the action of the novel revolves around Ethan's and Mattie's growing (inarticulate) love, Zeena's presence standing between them, and the tragic outcome.

Zeena does not actively hate, but behaves hatefully. Her illness, through which she controls others, is her main form of hatefulness, but so too is her character, built of nastiness, intimidation, and lack of concern for others. It is Ethan who is induced to hate. Thus, when Zeena was going to send Mattie away:

> Confused motions of rebellion stormed in [Ethan]. He was too young, too strong, too full of the sap of living, to submit so early to the destruction of his hopes. Must he wear out all his years on the side of a bitter, querulous woman? Other possibilities had been in him, possibilities sacrificed, one by one, to Zeena's narrowmindedness and ignorance. And what good had come of it? She was a hundred times bitterer and more discontented than when he had married her: the one pleasure left her was to inflict pain on him. All the healthy instincts of self-defense rose up in him against such waste. [p. 94]

And later, after he and Mattie had found words for their love:

> The words were like fragments torn from his heart. With them came the hated vision of the house he was going back to—of the stairs he would have to go up every night, of the woman who would wait for him there. And the sweetness of Mattie's avowal, the wild wonder of knowing at last that all that had happened to him had happened to her too, made the other vision more abhorrent, the other life more intolerable to return to. [p. 120]

And, in the most powerful instance, when Ethan had first learned of Zeena's intention to send Mattie away—Zeena

simply behaving in her way, interested in her care, quoting
what "the doctor says" is best for her:

> Ethan's hand dropped from the door-knob, which he had held
> clenched since he had drawn the door shut on Mattie. His
> wife's retort was like a knife cut across the sinews, and he felt
> suddenly weak and powerless. [p. 95]

> Ethan looked at her with loathing. She was no longer the
> listless creature who had lived at his side in a state of sullen
> self-absorption, but a mysterious, alien presence, an evil en-
> ergy, secreted from the long years of silent brooding. It was
> the sense of her helplessness that sharpened his antipathy.
> There had never been anything in her that one could appeal to;
> but as long as he could ignore and command he had remained
> indifferent. Now she had mastered him and he abhorred
> her. . . . She had taken everything else from him; and now she
> meant to take the one thing that made up for all the others. For
> a moment such a flame of hate rose in him that it ran down on
> his arm and he clenched his fist against her. He took a wild step
> forward and then stopped. [pp. 84–85]

Ethan, not a man who hates, comes to hate the woman
who hates without experiencing her own hating.

A fifth transformation is repression. The hate in the
subject is buried, alien, feared, only making itself known in
symptomatic acts, dreams, slips of the tongue—with perhaps
an occasional eruption, rapidly covered over and undone.
Reaction formation—goodness, kindness—may be more in
evidence.

And the sixth, and last, that has been evident to me is
repression coupled with masochistic suffering. The original
victim of hate is largely unaware of her own hate (although it
may or may not be evident to others), but experiences herself
as suffering at the hands of others. In this transformation, as I
have seen it, the suffering is not because the other is experi-

enced as rageful (like the early mother), or because one's own hate is experienced as an internal attack (as I described above), but the suffering is more subtly masochistic—feeling mistreated, deprived, ignored, or the like. Margaret Fitzpatrick-Hanly (1993) describes Charlotte Bronte's *Jane Eyre* in such terms. Treated abysmally in her childhood, she rages against it. But the rages are gone in her adult years, and she lives a life of service and sacrifice and, at times, suffering.

SUMMARY

I have described a particular setting for the development of one kind of hate—a seething, long-lived emotion that surfaces periodically in righteous and/or explosive rage, in masochistic suffering, or in hate induced in others, which derives in part from a sense of being treated in a devalued, thing-like way, and helplessness to affect this treatment. When I have seen this clinically, the source of the experience has been the quality of the mother's rage, making the child into an object, losing its personhood, and with the mother's becoming a stranger to the child. Some of the transformations that this rage undergoes, and its modes of appearance in adult patients, were also described.

REFERENCES

Balzac, H. de (1846). *Cousin Bette*. London: Penguin Books, 1965.

Bronte, C. (1847). *Jane Eyre*. London: Penguin Classics, 1985.

Euripides (413 B. C.). *Medea*. London: Penguin Classics, 1963.

——— (415 B. C.). *Elektra*. London: Penguin Classics, 1963.

Fitzpatrick-Hanly, M. (1993). Sadomasochism in Charlotte Bronte's *Jane Eyre*. *International Journal of Psycho-Analysis* 74:1049–1061.

Gaitskill, M. (1991). *Two Girls, Fat and Thin*. New York: Bantam, 1992.

Gordon, M. (1993). The deadly sins: Anger. *New York Times Book Review*, June 13, pp. 3, 31.

Ibsen, H. (1890). *Hedda Gabler*. In *Ibsen's Plays*. New York: Random House.

O'Neill, E. (1929, 1931). *Mourning Becomes Electra*. In *Nine Plays*. New York: Liveright, 1932.

Stead, C. (1940). *The Man Who Loved Children*. New York: Holt, 1965.

Strindberg, A. (1888). *Miss Julie*. In *Eight Famous Plays*. New York: Scribners, 1950.

Wharton, E. (1911). *Ethan Frome*. New York: Macmillan, 1987.

7

HATRED IN WOMEN: A CRITIQUE OF ITS ORIGINS AND EFFECTS

Discussion of Pine's Chapter "On the Origin and Evolution of a Species of Hate: A Clinical-Literary Excursion"

Dorothy E. Holmes, PH.D.

> Tell us what it is to be a woman so that we may
> know what it is to be a man . . .
> (Morrison, 1994, p. 29).

It is a pleasure to discuss Fred Pine's work, for he has been a mentor, teacher, and supervisor of mine, unknown to him. I have pondered his excellent work on my own, in study groups at my institute, and in classes I teach. And now, I am learning from him again with his excursion into the origins and evolution of a "species of hate." As discussant for this excursion, my job is to say what I have learned, what questions the trip left me with, and to make suggestions for further exploration.

Following Pine across time, from the fifth century B.C. to the present time, we find that hate has existed as an irreducible and inevitable affect. Pine's contribution here would be considerable even if his chapter had been limited to the taxonomy of hatred with which he has provided us. He identifies many important triggers to hatred: loss and consequent pain; sexual jealousy; a sense of injury and of righteousness; superego flaws that give permission for it and potentiate pleasure deriving from its expression; scorn; humiliation; oedipal conflict; the need to relieve self-hate; and the trigger that seems to come closest in his thinking to a cause, that is, frustration in the search for mother's love.

SELF-HATRED IN WOMEN

I will highlight two of the triggers identified by Pine: the need to relieve self-hate and frustration in the search for mother's love. In the matter of self-hate, my first long-term psychotherapy patient was a black woman who presented for treatment because she was afraid she was going to participate in the race riots that were ongoing in her city at the time she sought treatment. She relieved herself of this burden upon meeting me by facilely projecting onto me her self-loathing. That is, she attached it to my race (black), professional status (psychology intern), and gender (female) when, in the first appointment, she said, "Why did they [idealized, predominantly white, university hospital] give me you . . . you're black, a psychologist, and a woman!" Clearly, the patient was frightened that an external condition (riots) was going to coerce her to be in touch with and give violent expression to her aggression. The treatment saved her from the violence and permitted a safe, though at first defensive, experience of her aggression.

Unlike Pine's prototype of hatred in women, treatment of this woman didn't lead to discovery of a maternal root of her hatred. Given her strong yearnings for nurturance, probably there were such roots. If so, they remained defensively buried beneath her sense that the "system" failed her. The "system" was her experience of a racist white society, which she thought produced weak black men and which she also idealized. System issues for her were the available source of the loathing she turned on herself and projected onto me. I highlight this case to raise the possibility that there are cultural codeterminants of anyone's hatred that must be acknowledged in treatment. It may be that in some cases, such as the one just noted, the patient may limit the focus of treatment to such factors if they play a central role in maintaining adequacy of ego functioning and/or characterological stability.

The importance of frustrations in the search for mother's love to the development of hatred is emphasized by Pine. Specifically, in his discussion of O'Neill's *Mourning Becomes Electra*, he states, "Thus it is not the case that Lavinia is primarily in rivalry with the mother for the *father's* love, but is in rivalry with Orin and Brant for her *mother's* love. . . . The first failed relationship with the mother of infancy, hopelessly beyond the child's reach, underlies the subsequent hate." Thus hated and growing up to hate, Pine hypothesizes that women in particular then hate their daughters who are helpless to affect the experience of being hated by mother. Pine states, "These two features—being reduced and objectified and the helplessness to affect it—are the defining ones." Given the centrality of helplessness in Pine's theory, it is necessary that he clarify helplessness in terms of development and defense. That is, while in relative terms helplessness is a generalized state of infancy and early childhood, the human organism does not always stay helpless in the face of rages from parents except by the workings of superego functions and defense; witness some instances of matricide, an instance of which is presented below. Perhaps it is of the defensive function that Pine speaks when he says, "And so, not only does the child [being hated by the mother] feel not recognized by the mother, *but also fails to recognize the mother*" (italics added). It would be interesting to study what kinds of defenses are employed in cases where hatred is salient and chronic in parent–child relationships. I will review an additional perspective on the defensive function of helplessness later when I discuss possible theoretical underpinnings to Pine's view of the origins of hatred.

In addition to proposing the various origins of hatred summarized above, Pine also maps out for us six possible evolutionary changes in the course of hate. In its least evolved form, the hater acts most like the one by whom she was originally most hated, that is, the mother, in Pine's view. The remaining five transformations of hate are superego development of a sense of rightness that makes it possible to take pleasure in hating; a form in which "the hate is owned but dreaded"; the hater becomes hateful; the hating becomes repressed, erupting occasionally in symptoms; and repression over hatred may get reinforced by masochistic suffering.

Pine hypothesizes that the phenomenology, triggers, possible cause, and transformations of hate have a species-specific form in women, which bears repeating: Pine proffers that the affect of hating in women has as its central onset conditions "the daughter's encounter with her mother's repeated rages," and in that encounter the daughter is "being reduced and objectified and [is] helpless" to do anything about it. Pine cites these features as defining of the species of hate about which he is writing. Do I take him correctly to mean that when a woman hates, these are the irreducible underlying determinants, and does he mean to imply that the determinants of hate in men are different?

To the extent that a mother's hatred of a child is causal in the child's expressed hatred toward that mother and/or others, I believe the fate of male children who have been hated by their mothers must also be addressed. For example, I once evaluated for the courts a 19-year-old man who was facing sentencing for having killed his mother by repeatedly stabbing her and then burning her body. A well-documented history pointed to a soul-murdering, hate-filled hold the mother had on her son, including, even at age 19, routinely locking him in the house and frequently beating him. After one such beating, she demanded that he leave the house so that she could "entertain" her boyfriend. The son then fashioned a spear and the next time she hit him, he killed her. His explanation for burning her body was to be rid of her because as he stabbed his mother, she mockingly said that he would never be rid of her. This young man showed at least some of the attributes cited by Pine in his description of a a species of hate in women, that is, a repression of his hate reinforced by masochism, helplessness, and finally a breakdown of the repression and eruption of the symptom of murdering his mother. I raise this clinical vignette to suggest that clarification is needed of what there is in the hate described by Pine that makes it unique to mothers and daughters?

That there may be other sources of hate in women is addressed by Pine when he notes "the stories of women who hate because of being dominated by a world of men" and adds, "I have not seen this as a *primary* source of hate in female patients." I think we would benefit from knowing more of the basis on which Pine rests his case that the primary source of the hatred he describes in women is their interactions with their mothers, for he seems to make generous allowance that any sadistic regime can be a source of hate. Furthermore, although he states that he has not seen domination by men as a primary source of hate in female patients, his data source is English literature. To the extent that these data are adequate building blocks for his hypotheses, then to some extent he must be talking about women in general.

Is it possible that women who accurately locate sources of their hatred in the domination by men don't come to therapy as often as women who do not recognize this source, or that when they do come for treatment, their hatred is not as great a factor in their disturbance? I'm reminded here of a long-ago conversation with a great-aunt of mine who puzzled over the advent of the feminist movement. She wondered why women were expending so much effort to become equal to men when they had always been superior. In part the answer could be that our society does not easily permit a recognition of superiority in women.

I'm also reminded of a psychological study from the late 1960s that showed that blacks who developed accurate externalizing skills about the prevalence of racial discrimination in our society showed more ego strength than those who lacked such skills (Gurin et al. 1969). Shall we hypothesize similarly about women, that is, that women who accurately recognize sources of their hatred, including its onset in how they are treated by men, are healthier than women who do not have such recognition? Pine makes some points that are consistent with this possibility in his early comments on Christina Stead's *The Man who Loved Children* when he notes: "While Henny is able to see Sam as a big baby, . . . and while she never quite sees *his* hating and hatefulness, she nonetheless predominantly hates him *and her condition,* seen as the slavery and sexual bondage of women. Her hate is simmering and eruptive by turns." Pine goes on to describe this character's extremely pathological hatred, an important context of which is her *non*-recognition of her husband's hate of her.

It seems to me that Pine is saying that women, saddled with maternal hatred, perhaps in combination with a codeterminant of societal hatred in the form of domination by men, in turn hate, and particularly hate their daughters. Do the data sources used by Pine support his proposition? Let us examine some excerpts from his wide-ranging literature survey to find out. Dr. Pine's inclusion of Mary Gaitskill's *Two Girls, Fat and Thin* is intriguing. About the origins of Dorothy's hatred he says, "But here, in the surge of feelings and memories that floods her, we see not only the hatred of the father, but one of its simplest transformations—her hatred of herself, that is, *her identification with his hate of her*" (italics added). I think that Pine's main point here is to describe a transformation of hating in a woman. Nevertheless, he points directly to a source of hate for the woman in question. Is it not a primary source, that is, the woman's long-standing relationship with a father who hated her? Similarly, in utilizing Stead's *The Man Who Loved Children*, could Pine expand on his decision to make Henny's, not Sam's, hate his focus, inasmuch as he recognizes that "Sam's hate is clear to the reader"? Do not these examples clearly raise the possibility that in some instances, women who hate their daughters are hating them as displacements away from men who hated them and thereby spawned their hate?

Related to the possibility that daughters are objects of displacement for their mothers' hatred, another question I have for Pine is: How does he decide on what is derivative and what is primary? Again, with reference to Stead's work, he says, "We are . . . given to believe that Henny's hate is predominantly a product of her marriage to Sam." Sam is described as mercilessly teasing, intrusive, a believer in sadistic ideologies, and as egocentric. Do these qualities not fit the picture of the phenomenology of hatred that Pine attributes to women? When Pine says "we are . . . given to believe," is he doubting that Sam is an important source of Henny's hate? In hypothesizing that Henny's hate came from her own interactions with her mother, is parsimony being strained? Where did her mother's hate come from? What's primary? What's derivative?

Here, I'm reminded of Pine's use of O'Neill's *Mourning Becomes Electra* and Christine's and Lavinia's hate-filled relationship. Christine explains her hate thus: "You would understand if you were the wife of a man you hated." I think this passage supports a view that the hatred of some mothers for their daughters is secondary, that is, a displacement. Perhaps such a fact explains why a hated daughter doesn't feel the hate is really about anything specific to herself. That is, we could wonder whether the hate by the mother is the only major problem for the girl child who is its target. Perhaps it is at least as damaging—and as hate-inducing—for the girl that she is a mere stand-in for the really hated one toward whom her mother isn't free to act hatefully. And why not? Why murder and incest and displacement to daughters instead of the wife/ mother taking on her husband, responding in kind, or doing whatever is possible to contribute to the reduction of the hate from her husband or between them? Is it a case of women being constrained by a societal role assignment to preserve others, especially men? Or, is it the fact that rage/hate, as Kernberg (1993, p. 63) proffers, is "the essential affect around which clusters the complex affective formation of aggression as a drive"? In line with this question, we must raise the possibility that women's relationships to their mothers, and then to their daughters, and women's relationship to men are mere contexts, not causes, for the expression of a drive that is always looking for a venue in which to express itself.

A TALE OF TWO GENDERS?

As suggested in my comments on the role of men in literature cited by Pine, I think it important to speak to the development of hate in both genders. I'm wondering how Pine would address a commonly held view that mother is the target, not source, of hatred for females *and* males. Kernberg (1989) puts it best and succinctly:

> The child's pathologically intense pregenital and particularly oral aggression—whether its source is a reaction to frustration (Fairbarn, Winnicott), or derived from inborn aggression (Klein)—is projected onto the parental figures, especially mother, thus causing a paranoid distortion of the early parental images. Because the child projects predominantly oral-sadistic but also anal-sadistic impulses, the mother is

experienced as potentially dangerous, and the hatred of the
mother later expands to hatred of both parents. [p. 244]

Thus, we must consider that at least sometimes reports of
having been hated by one's mother are a projection of the
hatred male and female children originally had for their mothers. And, going as far back as the writings of Bibring (1953)
and Horney (1932), we know of the consideration that males
are hard-pressed not to hate women, as a condition and
consequence of the complicated process by which they give
up their mothers as love objects.

I will present a brief case description that I hope will
illustrate some of the difficulty in the topic before us. The
patient, who is 64 years old and nearing retirement as a
government worker, was divorced 17 years ago and is desperate to find a lasting love and to remarry. The patient came
to treatment because of depression related to repeated failure
in the attainment of these goals. An analysis of several years'
duration 10 years ago had eased the patient's social anxieties,
but hadn't led to ego changes consistent with the possibility of
making a lasting love relationship. The referring analyst had
thought this patient would profit from treatment with a
woman, and so the patient was referred to me and is being
seen in psychotherapy twice a week. The patient's early life
was characterized by strain trauma of a screeching, vindictive
mother who carped at her two children constantly, and if they
protested or defended themselves in any way, threatened to
kill herself. She was hate-filled and hateful and spewed her
hate freely on her children. The patient's father was chronically depressed, avoidant of the patient's mother, pleasant but
not involved with the patient, and late in life, when a postre-
tirement business venture collapsed, killed himself. The patient has a major narcissistic disturbance and expresses hate
toward any prospective partner; the patient is initially very
receptive to lovers who are in one dimension or another

unacceptable. As the potential for intimacy grows, so does the patient's alternating distancing and frank sadism toward the lover who inevitably is precipitously, sometimes cruelly dropped. I think this patient by history and approach to current significant others fits Pine's profile. There is only one catch: the patient is a man.

So, when hate of a mother toward her child is a significant factor and not just the child's projection, is it not likely that a mother can hate a son or a daughter? This hate can be derivative of other targets of the mother's rage; it can view the children as "safe" targets; it can find the children available as objects of gratification because it is basic to do so.

What are the theoretical underpinnings of Pine's theory of hatred? It seems to me to be an offshoot of an interpersonal psychology, given the emphasis he places on the mother's direct role in shaping her offspring's hatred. That is, at a descriptive level, Pine's views on the origins of hatred seem to accord with Sullivan (1953), who asserted absolutely that our personalities are understandable as "the relatively enduring pattern of recurrent interpersonal situations which characterize a human life" (pp. 110–111). Does Pine intend to adopt a Sullivanian point of view? How might he fit his theory into or argue for its parsimony in relation to other psychoanalytic models and other psychological frames focused on human helplessness? For example, how might he answer the claim of contemporary affect theory, as in Kernberg's assertion that a function of object relations is to activate affects, including hatred? From the point of view of structural theory, Pine speaks of "some flaw in the superego" as a structural condition that permits a person to feel he or she has the right to hate. How does he articulate this idea with more established points of view, such as has been formulated by Schafer (1960): "It is in failing to reach these goals [of adaptation achieved in part through identification with admired parents] that the ego feels inferior. . . . [such feelings of inferiority] correspond to feelings of loss of the superego's love, just as guilt corresponds to feelings of the superego's hatred" (pp. 178–179).

Apropos frames of reference particularly focused on conditions fostering helplessness, a full review requires at least a brief mention of the work of Seligmann (1975). Though a behaviorist, Seligmann addresses numerous processes by which an individual's agency (control) is given to or taken by another. These processes, if not essentially defensive, have a defensive function and lead to helplessness. As may be inferred from the previous discussion of the young man who murdered his mother and the female protagonists cited by Pine, the cost of giving up the helplessness may be murder.

I think it imperative in a theory such as Pine's to develop a point of view to account for those persons exposed to the kind of hatred described and who do *not* themselves come to hate as a predominant mode of expression. By what means? How does a child on the receiving end of hatred by mother become something other than one who hates? As psychoanalysts we know that strain traumas usually cause severe intrapsychic damage, but we also know that outcomes are complex and in some cases benign and even salutary. Thus, there is a scientific necessity for Pine to elaborate his theory to account for good enough outcomes. Without such elaboration, his theory could be mistaken for women bashing, and it could lead to an indiscriminate embrace of those feminist theories that *only* allow for an idealized view of women defined in terms of their commitment to mothering and all of the positive derivatives therefrom. In the matter of the origins of hatred, as in so many other issues pertaining to men and women, I believe Chodorow (1989) is correct when she says, "We need to develop an approach to gender that enables understandings . . . of the selves and object-relational patterns of men and women" (p. 198).

CONCLUSION

To the extent that a mother's hate of her daughter is causal in the daughter's hate, might we recognize it as *a* factor among many? Similarly, mustn't we recognize mothers as a common pathway in the formation of hate in women and men? I do not know what role my being a woman played in my being chosen to discuss Pine's chapter. In most instances, I hope that my gender per se is not a major factor in being asked to do intellectual tasks, but in this case perhaps the perspectives of both genders are important. Toni Morrison's lecture upon being awarded the Nobel Prize in literature is relevant here. In good allegorical form, she has some surly young men ask a blind old woman whose wisdom they at first did not recognize, "Tell us what it is to be a woman so that we may know what it is to be a man. What moves at the margin. What is it to have no home in this place. To be set adrift from the one you knew. What is it to live at the edge of towns that cannot bear your company" (1994, p. 29). Thanks to the conveners of this wonderful symposium and to the evocative and creative thinking of Fred Pine, we come a bit closer to understanding the origins of hatred—a force in the lives of all of us that threatens to set us adrift from one another. By bearing one another's company, man and woman together, perhaps we can understand.

REFERENCES

Bibring, G. (1953). On the "passing of the Oedipus complex" in a matriarchal family setting. In *Drives, Affects and Behavior: Essays in Honor of Marie Bonaparte*, ed. R. M. Loewenstein, pp. 278–284. New York: International Universities Press.

Chodorow, N. (1989). *Feminism and Psychoanalytic Theory*. New Haven: Yale University Press.

Gurin, P., Gurin, G., Lao, R., and Beatlie, M. (1969). Internal–external control in the motivational dynamics of Negro youth. *Journal of Social Issues* 25:29–54.

Horney, K. (1932). The dread of women. *International Journal of Psycho-Analysis* 13:348–360.

Kernberg, O. (1989). A theoretical frame for the study of sexual perversion. In *The Psychoanalytic Core: Essays in Honor of Leo Rangell, M. D.*, ed. H. Blum, E. Weinshel, and F. Rodman, pp. 243–263. New York: International Universities Press.

_____ (1993). The psychopathology of hatred. In *Rage, Power, and Aggression*, ed. R. Glick, and S. Roose, pp. 61–79. New Haven: Yale University Press.

Morrison, T. (1994). *The Nobel Lecture in Literature, 1993*. New York: Knopf.

Schafer, R. (1960). The loving and beloved superego in Freud's structural theory. *Psychoanalytic Study of the Child* 15:163–188. New York: International Universities Press.

Seligmann, M. (1975). *Helplessness: On Depression, Development and Death*. San Francisco: Freeman.

Sullivan, H. S. (1953). *The Interpersonal Theory of Psychiatry*. New York: Norton.

8

HATE AND DEVELOPMENTAL SEQUENCES AND GROUP DYNAMICS: CONCLUDING REFLECTIONS

Peter B. Neubauer, M.D.

T his chapter discusses the conditions or characteristics that determine the change from aggression to hate and from hate to violence. The primary force of hate is drive related, but this does not apply to all conditions; the threat to the integrity of the ego or superego may lead to a splitting of the good and the bad, and therefore to hate. This splitting may then secondarily mobilize aggressive strivings to ward off and to defend against the external or internal danger.

It is this complex structural interplay, among other factors, that may be responsible for the limited attention we have paid to the topic of hate, and it reminds us of the few studies of the state of love. It is self-evident that aggression, filtered through ego and superego regulations, may be expressed by the competition with the object or the control or the submission of the object. I assume that during the state of hate, the ego-superego accepts the elimination or destruction of the object, an object that has become too dangerous for the integrity of the psychic structure, for the self. I would add this to

Fred Pine's formulation that "hate . . . is a long-lasting and widespread seething state, occasionally breaking through to the surface in rage, sadism, or subtler forms of hatefulness." Does "widespread" refer to the variations of hate or to the invasive effect of hate on all the agencies of the mind?

FROM HATE TO VIOLENCE

Under which conditions does hate lead to acts of violence? This simple question demands that we consider various conditions of the internal life in interaction with environmental factors.

In explaining psychopathology, we explore the balance between the drives or whether one dominates the other so that an appropriate fusion cannot take place. We may think of the weakened ego that is unable to defend against undue drive influences, or a weakened superego that gives insufficient support to the ego. In terms of object relations, we assume that a libidinal object cathexis or constancy is not available to regulate the internalized representation between object and self. Freud (1925) states:

> The function of judgement is concerned in the main with two sorts of decisions. It affirms or disaffirms the possession by a thing of a particular attribute; and it asserts or disputes that a presentation has an existence in reality. The attribute to be decided about may have originally been good or bad, useful or harmful. Expressed in the language of the oldest—the oral—instinctual impulses, the judgement is: "I should like to eat this" or "I should like to spit it out" . . . The original pleasure-ego wants to introject into itself everything that is bad. The other sort of decision . . . is a concern of the definitive reality-ego, which develops out of the initial pleasure-ego. It is, we see, once more a question of external and internal. [pp. 236–237]

What is important is his proposition that the ego from the beginning takes into itself what supports its function and expels what interferes with it. We must assume that when there is a state of hate, then the real world and the internal world cannot any longer be coordinated; then there is a rupture and externalization, projection and displacement places the internal world outside.

When we consider the developmental processes as a guide, we can easily assign the role of hate to each stage of development: the oral incorporation, the anal expulsion, the phallic reaction to castration, the oedipal hate against the rival, and so on.

Sandler and Rosenblatt (1962) propose that the internal world includes the internalized objects as well as those objects created by fantasies and wishes; each influences the other and each affects the perception of the outer reality, then the hate of the reality object is influenced by both. We have to differentiate those functions that repeat the past experiences from those that stem from the internal construction of wishes, fears, and fantasies.

From this point of view, let us examine the developmental sequences as proposed by Margaret Mahler. Her studies of the first three years of life inform us that mental life could be understood as being a negotiation between the need and wish to be united and the forces that strive toward individuation, self-fulfillment, and following an independent path. The projection of man's fate throughout life can be understood as a struggle to balance these two forces—the narcissistic love versus the object love.

During the practicing subphase, the *functions-lust* (i.e., the pleasure of ego in exercising a newly acquired skill) is fired by aggressive strivings in the pursuit of separation-individuation. There is the negativism that demands self-control and a degree of early autonomy. It is not achieved by yielding either to love or to control, but by the assertion of independence. There is too much passive-aggressive play, with temper tantrums, the fear of being autonomous, and the fear of being alone or of giving up ego faculties to explore the environment. The earlier turning away from the stranger, which supports the bonding to the object, is not challenged by curiosity to explore new things. When the bonding becomes a danger by mitigating the aggressive practicing of new skills involving the inner and outer territories, then the early turning against the object can become excessive.

I am referring to these well-known conditions in order to place our topic within these developmental conflicts and to show that aggression can then be transformed to hate. This duality between the forward momentum toward individuation and the repressive wish to maintain the object finds a dramatic expression during the rapprochement subphase. As the vulnerability is heightened, there is a change of mood, of the affect, and we assume with it there must be a struggle between the internalized and internal object representation and the self-representation. The fear of the loss of the love of the object and the search for the mother is also experienced as a regressive return. Now there is a deepening of the wish for reunion side by side with the fear of reengulfment.

There is a struggle for a balance between distancing, separateness, and closeness. There is a transitional space in which this interactive dilemma leads to further differentiation between the object and self, with the accompanying projection and projective identification. Attachment preserves safety although with an accompanying threat to the evolvement of the self. Distancing furthers differentiation, but also engenders the fear of losing the object.

We know from our clinical data that the fear of the loss of love either evokes a sense of unworthiness, a turning against the object or away from the object, aggression against the object, or mourning for the object. Thus it seems whether we examine our topic from a structural or object relational point of view, love and hate are part of the matrix of the human developmental condition.

GAMES CHILDEN PLAY

The play of children gives ample evidence of aggression, destruction, re-creation, and resurrection. While the content will change according to the developmental stage, the theme of aggression with destruction can be seen in the throwing away of the object and the peek-a-boo game, the crashing of the train and the repeated destruction of the block tower, and the killing of the soldiers on the battlefield and their revival. Play, fantasizing, daydreams, and unconscious fantasies have an organizing influence on mental function. In *Creative Writers and Day-Dreaming* Freud (1908) writes:

> Might we not say that every child at play behaves like a creative writer, in that he creates a world of his own or, rather, rearranges the things of his world in a way that pleases him? It would be wrong to think he does not take that world seriously . . . The opposite of play is not what is serious but what is real. In spite of all the emotion with which he cathects his world of play, the child distinguishes it quite well from reality; and he likes to link his imagined objects and situations to the tangible things of the real world. This linking is all that differentiates the child's play from "phantasysing" . . . As people grow up . . . they cease to play, and they seem to give up the yield of pleasure which they gained from playing. But whoever understands the human mind knows that hardly anything is harder for a man to give up [than] a pleasure which he has once experienced . . . What appears to be a renunciation is really the formation of a substitute or surrogate. In the same way, the growing child, when he stops playing, gives up nothing but the link with real objects; instead of *playing*, he now *phantasizes*. He builds castles in the air and creates what are called *day-dreams*. [pp. 143–144, 145]

This quotation illuminates the differential role the ego plays with wishes that demand to be expressed. When the mind is unable to control irrational wishes, when the ego cannot face conflict, it returns to defensive maneuvers to keep the fantasies repressed, which then have an organizing influence as they retain infantile characteristics.

During latency, as the child widens his relationships from the family to peers, he also proceeds from play to games. In play, subjectively determined wishes and fantasies seek new expressions, conflicts seek new solutions, passivity is changed to activity, and the endless repetition of the play theme allows a piecemeal mastery of conflicts and the building of new psychic structure. What is important is the recognition of the significance in the step from play to games, when the rules of conduct and conditions of competition are shared and accepted. This transformation during latency supports the ego's increasing mastery through the dominance of the reality principle. Intragroup aggression cannot be tolerated; it has to yield to the formation of the team. Thus group formation tames drive expression.

It is noteworthy that the games of war that the latency child in therapy constructs do not often specify the reason why the enemy has to be defeated. Whether the child arranges the war scenes between the cowboys and Indians or between the Nazis and the American forces, the good and bad are divided, needing no further explanation; the child does not specify the reason why he selects this particular enemy. Whatever the underlying fantasies may be, he wants to win the battle. He organizes his troops, and he resurrects the killed in order to continue the fight to subdue the enemy. The exercise of fighting, the practicing of being active to avoid passivity seems to be in the foreground of wishes.

The play of the preoedipal and oedipal child reveals a subjective enemy, feared for personal reasons, and designated as a ghost, the wicked witch, the lion under the bed, the robber in the hall. These figures represent the child's early fantasy life and the displacement of the primary objects by symbolic powerful images.

The adolescent, in contrast, insists on the designation of who is right and who is wrong and what is right and what is wrong. By shaping of an ideology, a search for clarity for the outer and inner identity, the formation of an enduring self takes place with a sharper profiling of new self-object images. It is during adolescence that so much can be gained by belonging to a group, even if submission to the group ideology interferes with the fermentation of the individuality of each member. Here is the link to group and mass psychology.

A short case vignette will illustrate some of these factors. The patient has been married for 4 years, has one child, and he and his wife think that the marriage cannot be maintained. They love each other; they have left each other, but they have always returned to one another with renewed longing. They have a passionate sex life. He has never found another woman who has aroused him erotically with as much intensity. He feels this will continue throughout their lives. Shortly after they were married, he suggested engaging in a ménage à trois. She readily agreed and they eventually invited another man, a casual friend, to join their sexual explorations. The patient assured me immediately that he is not gay. After that event his wife berated him, criticized him, and finally attacked him physically, declaring that she hated him, that she cannot love him any longer. This scene repeated itself many times. After her outburst and her violence, they fell into each other's arms and had their mutually passionate erotic reunion. He revealed that his wife had been seduced by her father with whom she had sex for many years during adolescence. She married during her college years. She was quite happy with the patient until he suggested the ménage à trois. The patient never realized that his suggestion had provoked her to reenact her experience with her father, with the same shame and excitement she had endured during her adolescence. He used the ménage à trois to satisfy his oedipal rivalry for he arranged the scene so that he was always the superior lover, and that she would always prefer him. The victorious repossession of his wife stimulated his erotic longings; she will always be his. This interlocking of their oedipal wishes and fears led to a continuous drama—a Greek drama. Instead of being rescued by her husband, protected from her own memories, his wife accused him of using her for his own excitement. The loss of love turned into hate and violent aggression. The marriage counselor advised them to refrain from sexual activities in order to interrupt her violent outbursts.

This case history confirms Fred Pine's position that "there are instances that might be relations between the sexes as a second version of some earlier hate-inducing relationship that is at the heart of the phenomenon. . . . Clinically, I have seen repeated eruption of rage as well as transformations of it, all with the original historical context."

THE ARENA OF GROUP PSYCHOLOGY

I shall now turn to a topic that Blum, in his wide-ranging discourse, has referred to, namely, the group and mass psychology activities that demonstrate so clearly how hate can be transformed into violence.

The individual in the group can commit acts of violence that he could never do alone. What are the conditions that dispose him to change aggression to hate and to violence? Hartmann (1958) says,

The social norms which the child adopts only partly coincide with the rewards and punishments he will actually receive from society in later life. These value hierarchies may serve as switching stations or crystallization points. . . . The significance of such value hierarchies formed in the individual varies according to the structure of the society in which they arise. . . . fitting together, the synthetic function must be supraordinate to the regulation by the external world. Otherwise, as Freud quotes Goethe, "reason becomes unreason, kindness torment." [p. 54].

In the name of "higher" group goals, which supersede individual interests, cruelties are committed against others without guilt or remorse. The American pioneers, striving to establish their community, their values, and their way of life, were ruthless in the elimination of the alien, native population. The Crusaders ravaged Europe on the way to "liberate" the holy places, and in the name of purity of the nation, one justifies "ethnic cleansing."

As Neubauer (1992) says,

It is well-known that belonging to a group influences the individual's independent decision faculty. One accepts the group code and assigns to the leader or the group the moral standards. Freud argued convincingly that the individual superego could easily lose the courage of its conviction when subjected to peer pressure and demagoguery. Morality can easily get lost in the crowd and be replaced by standards new or even alien to the individual in the group. One reason why this abandonment seems to come too easily is the notion that one returns to a stage of normal development, and with it a false sense of well-being is achieved. To free oneself from the pressure of one's own conscience *and* thereby achieve the acceptance of and belonging to others gives comfort, particularly when the conscience is appeased, when the group adheres to a new ideology which transcends the individual for the good of all. Thus, what is heterogeneous is submerged in what is homogeneous and the unconscious foundations, which are similar in everyone, stand exposed to view.

Since the critical faculty is relinquished, the irrational has open reign. Thus, the earlier magical power is tapped with a belief in words and the power of suggestion. Thus the mutual tie between members of a group is in the nature of an identification based upon an important emotional quality. This is a return to an earlier stage in life when the loved person enjoyed freedom from criticism, while the others, the outsiders, were condemned. Freud (1921) has outlined these factors in his *Group Psychology and the Analysis of the Ego*.

The de-structuralization by the weakening of the superego and the ego is paralleled by de-differentiation and de-individuation. The recognition of shading of opinions leads to a global assessment of the polarization between the good and the bad, the familiar and the strange, the loved and the hated. This is seen in the psychic life of young children. De-individuation leads to the pleasure of symbiosis, to the uncritical belonging. When the idea of pure blood was introduced, no compromise could be tolerated; impurity was the danger, the stranger in the midst of society, and had to be eliminated.

The return to symbiotic bonding is accompanied by a feeling of elation, the discarding of higher demands changed the *"Unlust in der Kultur"* to the *"Lust in der Unkultur."* But it is also clear that the return to the earlier undifferentiated bonding evokes danger, the anticipation of the rupture of the unity, and therefore is compelled to be reconfirmed. To be alerted to the external dangers, one must be ready to destroy, for there is the fear of being destroyed. Thus there is the inevitable dance with death. The spell of the magic power endows the enemy with power and the leader is given magic power that one does not dare to doubt. The group has to turn against the internal danger with ruthless force in order to maintain its fragile cohesion. The baby turns away from the stranger, but is equally anxious and disturbed when the symbiotic partner separates. These analogies to early development also reveal that the normal baby in a normal environment can rely on his developmental pull, on his capacity to learn that the fear will pass and an internal tolerance will limit the level of frustration. The pathological group condition cannot lean on progression, and the regression will reveal the conflict that can only be resolved when development is permitted to proceed again. During the regressed state of a totalitarian group, one does not learn from those who oppose it, for opposition only reinforces the group cohesion and the irrationality does not yield to reality.

There are many studies of group formation, of the various roles of the individual in the group, and of the influence of the group on the individual. Equal attention should be paid to the process of recovery, of the effect of the dissolution of a group or a movement on the individual. How does one proceed when the regressive forces are ruptured, when the ego ideal is shattered, when the symbiosis is dissolved? How does one recover from that illness? Is there a sense of mourning, of confusion? And for how long? How does the individual conscience establish again a moral force that regulates behavior? Who wishes that the old glory will return and who will slowly awaken to face reality? One could assume that during this period of recovery, the emerging superego may assert its voice and engender a sense of guilt. But it also may be that the voice of the superego may lead toward a repression of the experiences during the regressed state or another voice may justify the previous actions that were undertaken not for the benefit of the individual, but for the survival and elevation of the group. Is the individual then concerned that he or she fell before the contaminating forces, that one did not stand up against the group, when so many others did? I wish there were more information about the steps that lead toward the progressively reinstated autonomy of function.

UNANSWERED QUESTIONS

Where is the influence of the memories of that deviant past? Where are the nightmares revealing the need for the punish-

ment of atrocities committed or tolerated? There are no satisfactory answers available, and in a more schematic way we
may consider a number of options to be explored.

Does the submergence of superego function to the group
ideal eliminate guilt not only during the group cohesion but
also after it is dissolved? Since there is no "individual" guilt, it
cannot be recaptured later. Since group action is experienced
outside of conflicts, as part of a generally acceptable and
demanded morality, the memories of these experiences cannot
revive a sense of guilt that has never existed. One could rather
postulate a national or group guilt.

There is a *Verleugnung*, a negation of the implication of
present and past action, a defensive maneuver to protect pain
from ego and superego functions. The absence of guilt that
should influence future behavior is therefore repressed. If it
has become unconscious, should we not then have manifestation of its underground existence, by reaction formation or by
its shaping of character or symptom formation? Can we
postulate unconscious guilt that remains silent, a guilt about
massive hostile aggression that leads to massive destruction of
other human beings? How is it to be understood that so many
individuals return later to behavior expected from "normal"
citizens, that one could not recognize by their later actions the
extent to which they have violated human life? When we find
in the anamneses of our patients that a whole period of their
life is inaccessible to consciousness, is isolated from the rest of
their development—where there is such an absence of memories of their early childhood or adolescence, we assume it is
the result of unbearable psychic pain. We also expect that
these repressed experiences will affect present functioning, that there will be some form of enactment or defensive
attitude of those areas that touch on the previous painful
conditions. Do we have such accounts from the analysis of
patients who participated in national group activities of hostile aggression? Or do we find an attitude that since everyone

was guilty, no one alone is burdened to carry the post-event guilt, even when the idealized aim and justification for destruction no longer exists? Does this promote the further emotional distancing from guilt with a defense that is not only precludes feeling guilty for crimes but also is committed to oppose the judgment of the world that threatens the inner equilibrium and the return to a more stable self-representation. To this defense against guilt there may be added the defense against shame, and the latter may replace the former.

Thus, there is a difference between the regression under the auspices of the ego, regression as a retreat from unacceptable new conflicts, and group-determined regression that is ego syntonic and adaptive during the life of the group.

SUMMARY

I have outlined the transition from aggression to hate and from hate to violence. I have reviewed the developmental steps, structural considerations, and Mahler's separation-individuation sequences in order to demonstrate the confluence of psychic conditions that underlie aggression and hate. I have referred to the differences between individual pathology and group dynamics that lead to hate and violence. These are only some factors to be considered for our discussion. There are many areas as yet uncharted.

REFERENCES

Freud, S. (1908). Creative writers and Daydreaming *Standard Edition* 9:143–153.

———— (1921). Group psychology and the analysis of the ego. *Standard Edition* 18:65–143.

———— (1925). Negation *Standard Edition* 19:233–239.

Hartmann, H. (1958). *Ego Psychology and the Problem of Adaptation.* New York: International Universities Press.

Neubauer, P. B. (1992). *Various expressions of aggression in early childhood.* Presented at the Freud Gesellschaft 25th Year Symposium, Vienna.

Sandler, J., and Rosenblatt, B. (1962). The concept of the representational world. *Psychoanalytic Study of the Child* 17:128–145. New York: International Universities Press.

Index

165